LITTLE RAILWAYS OF THE WORLD

LITTLE RAILWAYS
OF THE WORLD

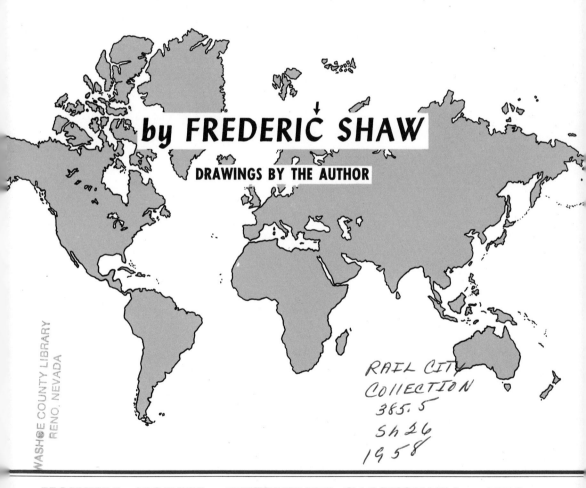

by FREDERIC SHAW

DRAWINGS BY THE AUTHOR

HOWELL-NORTH · BERKELEY, CALIFORNIA · 1958

Published by the HOWELL - NORTH PRESS
1050 Parker Street, Berkeley 10, California

*Printed and bound in the United States of
America by the publisher.*

To

ALBERT S. CAMPBELL

With Gratitude

LITTLE RAILWAYS OF THE WORLD

FOREWORD

Smoke Rings

Those of us who regret the passing of the Age of Steam will take heart at the durable nature of some of the world's miniature railways. In the United States particularly, the small steam locomotives are often our only reminder that once their big prototypes were a commonplace on the railroads of the nation. In many foreign lands, the miniature steam locomotive has had a better chance of survival; but they disappear one by one until only a few are left, preserved in the case of Britain by Railway Societies and others. These reawaken our interest in the part the steam engine once played in the world of commerce and in our daily lives.

Going on a train journey was always an adventure. And in the world today there are still a few miniature railways, whether they be common carriers, private lines or recreational projects, where the more leisurely pleasures of going on a train journey can still be experienced.

In the belief that there must be many people who would like to share with me over half a century of travel, both actual and armchair, on some of these outstanding miniature railways of the world, I have set down in the following pages the story of the roads themselves and the men who had much to do with them.

FREDERIC SHAW, A.I.A.

June 5, 1958

Sausalito, California

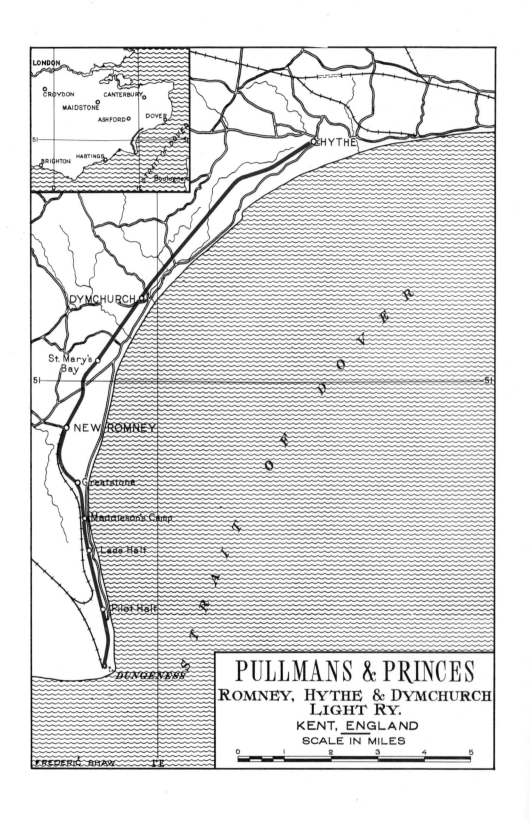

LONDON

CROYDON   CANTERBURY
    MAIDSTONE
        ASHFORD   DOVER

51

    BRIGHTON   HASTINGS

                Boulogne

HYTHE

DYMCHURCH

St. Mary's
Bay

51   51

NEW ROMNEY

    Greatstone

    Maddieson's Camp

    Lade Halt

STRAIT OF DOVER

    Pilot Halt

    DUNGENESS

FREDERIC SHAW

PULLMANS & PRINCES
ROMNEY, HYTHE & DYMCHURCH
LIGHT RY.
KENT, ENGLAND
SCALE IN MILES

0   1   2   3   4   5

CHAPTER I

PULLMANS AND PRINCES

The Romney, Hythe and Dymchurch Light Railway

FROM THE TIME Christopher Morley as an Oxford Rhodes scholar saw a locomotive named "Sir Bors de Ganis", visiting Americans have ever remarked on the romance of British practice and performance. To one accustomed to the uniformly drab appearance of the steam locomotive in the United States, it is something of an experience to stand by the "permanent way", as the Briton calls it, and watch the colorful trains go by. What the equipment lacks in size by American standards is amply compensated for by the names of the express trains and the delightful coloring of the locomotive and passenger equipment. Who can dismiss the urge to go for a train ride when the "Flying Scotsman", "The Cornish Riviera" or the "Talisman" go thundering by?

In the realm of miniature railroading, Britain has matched her standard gauges for design and engineering craftsmanship, and one of her most outstanding lines is the Romney, Hythe and Dymchurch Light Railway in Kent. Something in this part of England — the Kentish beaches and the storied Romney Marsh — lends itself to a smaller scheme of things. A perfect replica of a main line engine whose smokestack reaches only to the engineer's shoulder does not seem out of place. The minuscule system of stations, bridges, signals, track, motive power and rolling stock is a world more real than our own workaday existence.

Most of the credit for its creation must go to one man, an ex-racing motorist. This man, Captain J. E. P. Howey, saw in the early 1920's the growing popularity of the beaches between Hythe and New Romney and a lack of transportation to serve the vacationers. The Romney Marsh itself lies like a green sea, bounded on one side by the English Channel and on the other by the bastions of the ancient Cinque Ports whose cliffs and water gates suggest the Elizabethan era when the first Queen of that name could sail her barge to their very portals. The marshes were drained and became good pasture but they are still wild and sea-haunted.

1

Capt. J. E. P. Howey, original builder, present owner of the Romney, Hythe & Dymchurch Light Ry. It is often called "The Line That Jack Built."

Mr. George A. Barlow, senior engineer on the Romney line, looking out at you from the engine he habitually drives, the handsome *Green Goddess*.

Handsome Canadian Pacific type 4-6-2- *Doctor Syn* at the head of a passenger consist, crossing the largest double-track bridge over one of the numerous canals of Romney Marsh.

Passenger consist headed by locomotive *Northern Chief*, 4-6-2, rounding the loop at Dungeness Light. The train is known as the "Marshlander."

A double-header with *Green Goddess* in the lead, driver Barlow "up", approaching Dungeness Light, hauling most of the road's passenger rolling stock.

Across this marsh by the Channel, Howey decided to build his miniature railroad. He had already gained valuable experience in the operation of a fifteen-inch-gauge line on the grounds of his estate, Staughton Manor, in Huntingdonshire.

The Southern Railway learned of Howey's interest and offered him assistance. It was in their own interest to link the standard gauge terminals at New Romney and Hythe respectively. A company was formed under the Light Railway Acts of 1898 after the customary public enquiry into its need and usefulness, and construction work started in January, 1926.

Howey selected the fifteen-inch gauge of his Staughton Manor line — the "minimum gauge", as British railroaders term it — and every hour of the construction period from January 1926 to the summer of 1927, he was on the job, supervising every detail of the track construction, signaling, stations and bridges. Rail, which weighed 24 lbs. per yard, was laid in the American manner, spiked directly to the 3-foot long sleepers (ties) and not in chairs, the usual European method. Rail joints were staggered, also a departure from European practice, to minimize danger to trains. A 3-inch layer of shingle ballast, obtained locally, formed the track's foundation. Grades in this flat countryside were virtually non-existent and the sharpest curve was of 462 feet radius. In those days an extension of the line to Sandling Junction on the standard gauge London-Folkestone route was contemplated and two powerful little engines were bought, built specially to cope with the stiff grades involved. But the project was abandoned as too expensive and the line extended southwards to Dungeness Lighthouse instead.

The mileage of the little road thus became 13¾ of double track throughout, except for the loop at Dungeness, where the tracks separated.

Trains were, and still are, operated under Ministry of Transport requirements, which governs the operations of all British railroads. Divided into "blocks", trains are moved in accordance with the signaling. Inasmuch as with the exception of the Dungeness loop the entire line is double tracked, there is practically no danger of collision incident to single track operation. All trains carry tail light or tailboards, day and night.

Stations on this Lilliput system might be expected to be of a whistle stop variety. Nothing could be farther from the truth. The three main stations at New Romney, Hythe and Dymchurch are imposing structures with roofs extending over the tracks. The largest station, Hythe, has four platform tracks and conforms in every respect to a main line terminal of the standard gauges. In all respects — signals, freight yards, engine houses, turntables and bridges — the Romney, Hythe and Dymchurch Light Railway is a replica of its bigger proto-types.

All this sets the scene for the unique motive equipment and rolling stock. The railroad has nine steam locomotives, seven of which are Pacific type 4-6-2, the other two being of Mountain type 4-8-2. When first constructed, two of the engines had three cylinders instead of the conventional two. But in 1935 and 1937 respectively, the locomotives in question — No. 7 *Typhoon* and No. 8 *Hurricane* — the three cylinders were supplanted by two-cylinder blocks. Locomotives No. 9 and No. 10 were radical departures from the usual clean lines of the British engine, for they were patterned after the Canadian Pacific motive equipment which follows closely American design in that they have pilots ("cow-catchers"), Vanderbilt type tenders and bells. All locomotives have copper fire boxes, are equipped with superheaters which reduce fuel consumption and increase efficiency generally. They operate under a head of 180 lbs. of steam, Welsh coal being used as fuel. The wagon top boilers are false, this being accomplished by the lagging at the firebox end. The boilers are actually straight cylinders. Today, these handsome locomotives remain a fine memorial to their designer, the late Henry Greenly, who had pioneered the fifteen-inch steam locomo-tive on other European miniature systems, particularly the Ravenglass and Eskdale, which is dealt with in another chapter.

If technicalities crowd these early paragraphs, it is only because they provide an interesting backdrop for the performance of this little line and the high standards it maintains. The locomotives average 10,000 miles of travel each season and the original Pacifics have already covered a quarter million miles. It is fortunate that this stud was so substantially built, otherwise the economy of the Romney Railway might be different today. The engines cost on an average £1,600 ($7,680 at the then rate of exchange), and the present-day cost would probable be in excess of £8,000.

Before leaving the motive power and rolling stock, mention should be made of the "pullman" cars. Pullman is a term applied, in British railway usage, to non-compartmentalized coaches whose appointments include chair seats. They are almost standard equipment on the line. Originally painted in a blue and cream livery with a heraldic emblem to enhance the design, Pullmans now appear in a soft green which has

This is as comprehensive a photo of 15″ gauge steam locomotives in process of manufacture as could be devised. Here are four Pacific types and one mountain type in various stages of construction in the shops of Davey, Paxman & Co., Ltd. Note lone engine truck in lower left, two tenders upside down, and chassis on right of the young man.

Davey, Paxman & Co. Ltd.

Nearing completion in the Davey, Paxman shops and still on the test stand, one of the Pacific locomotives is depicted about ready for its finishing touches.

© *Dr. P. Ransome-Wallis*

This emblem adorns the sides of passenger cars of the R. H. & D. Ry. It is colorful and brilliant.

Locomotive No. 7, *Typhoon,* with Driver Barlow "up" about to leave New Romney engine terminal in October, 1947.

Queen Elizabeth, Prince Phillip immediately behind, Prince Charles and Princess Anne say "Goodbye" to senior engineer George A. Barlow, driver of the locomotive *Hurricane* at Hythe Sta. after the royal family completed its ride.

Passing trains at the end of double track exchanging the "staff" which authorized the rightful train to move out onto the single track of the main. Locomotive *Southern Maid*, 4-6-2, on the right.

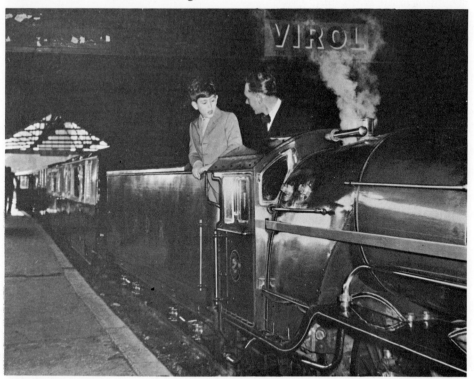

Prince Charles discusses with engineer George A. Barlow his reactions to a trip on the engine's footplate. Taken at Hythe Station.

greater weathering qualities in the strong sea air of Kent. For the fresh-air fiend — and who has not heard of the British passenger whose first thought on entering a compartment is to throw open the windows even on the coldest day? — there are semi-open coaches available.

The 2nd World War found the Romney Railway in one of the most exposed parts of the "invasion coast". In June 1940, the line was requisitioned by the Army and an armored mobile anti-aircraft train was soon patrolling the deserted vacationland beaches. Hauled by powerful *Hercules,* the train saw much action, since it was an avowed target of Goering's Luftwaffe. *Hercules* suffered slight bomb damage, but *Doctor Syn* ("sin") and a nine-car train were less lucky. The Luftwaffe scored a near miss on the track one dark night and the weakened line failed to hold a heavily laden Army train steaming along just after the raid. *Doctor Syn* and the cars tumbled into the huge crater. It is an ironical fact, however, that more damage was done to the line by British troops than by enemy attacks. Unaccustomed to the methods of working a miniature road, the soldiers left the railway in a deplorable condition at war's end.

Perhaps the most important work performed by the world's smallest public railway was the part it played in the Allied invasion of the Normandy beaches in 1944. PLUTO — or "The pipeline under the ocean" — was one of the logistical keys in supplying the Allied troops. Many miles of steel pipe and hundreds of technicians and troops engaged in this work were transported by the railway. Many of the pipe sections were welded together on the platform of New Romney station, converted into a temporary welding shop. The pipeline between Littlestone on the English coast and Bologne on the French coast supplied millions of gallons of gasoline to the invasion forces.

When the line was turned back to the owners in January 1946, a formidable task faced the operatives. Nothing short of complete renewal of the track was necessary. Equipment had been smashed and neglect lay like a blight over everything else. The rebirth of the line was nothing short of a miracle. Railroading breeds a peculiar type of enthusiasm, and repairs, reconstruction and rebuilding proceeded at such a pace, aided by Italian POW's, that by the close of the 1946 summer season, more than 250,000 passengers had been carried. By March 21, 1947, all rehabilitation of the system was completed and a grand opening staged.

In recent years, the railway has had to fight the greatest battle of all — the battle of rising costs. Economies have had to be effected in a way that will not militate against the chances of this promotion-minded little road attracting an increasing number of visitors each year. Promotion is the lifeblood of any enterprise, and the route of "Pullmans and Princes" legitimately gets more than its share of the news.

In 1948, branch delegates of the National Union of Railwaymen held a conference at Hastings, a special train having been scheduled for them to run non-stop from Dungeness to Hythe, a distance of 13.8 miles. The Romney, Hythe and Dymchurch special made the run "right on the advertised". It was a triple-header — *Green Goddess* in the lead, coupled to the 4-6-2 *Typhoon* and the 4-8-2 *Hurricane,* the veteran of the armored train. George A. Barlow, engineer of the *Green Goddess,* relates the story:

> "I was on the first engine. Surely this was a world record—four hundred fifty-eight people in one covered train of forty-seven coaches on 15-inch track. As we roared through New Romney with three chimneys 'talking' under the station roof, it must have been a sight for bystanders. I can tell you that looking back from the front engine was a thrill—particularly on the curves!"

Senior Engineer Barlow discussed the finer points of railroading with none other than Prince Charles. The son of Queen Elizabeth II and the heir to the British throne climbed into the cab of the *Hurricane* at Botolph's Bridge during the run of a special Royal train in March, 1957. His sister, Princess Anne, had sat on a cushion in the corner of the footplate. Her remarks had been confined to a child's admiration of the "lovely engine"; but Prince Charles, knowing his father, the Duke of Edinburgh, had acted as fireman on the *Hurricane* for the first part of the journey, wanted to take a more active part. Engineer Barlow instructed his royal apprentice in the art of tooting the whistle which Prince Charles blew lustily at every grade crossing, signal and group of photographers along the line.

The engines — indeed the whole system — has a storybook quality no child can resist. Each engineer keeps his own locomotive and is responsible for its maintenance and cleaning, and assists in any major overhaul during the winter. A certain latitude is allowed each man regarding details. For example, he can, within limits, choose his own setting for the piston valves. He can have smoke deflectors fitted if he likes, or a raised lip on the stack. Even the colors are different. The three Pacifics, Nos. 1, 2 and 7, are painted malachite green; the Pacific No. 3 is "Brighton" umber; No. 8 is Caledonian blue; the Canadian 4-6-2 No. 9 is painted maroon; Canadian 4-6-2 No. 10 is green with maroon wheels; 4-8-2 No. 5 is "Brighton" umber again; and 4-8-2 No. 6 is black.

One of the few grade crossings on the Romney line. Engineers are required to stand up on the footplate in such instances, slow down the train's speed and be alert to approaching vehicles.

The crack highspeed train *Bluecoaster* leaving Hythe, pulled by locomotive No. 8, *Hurricane,* on a bright, sunny day by the Straits of Dover.

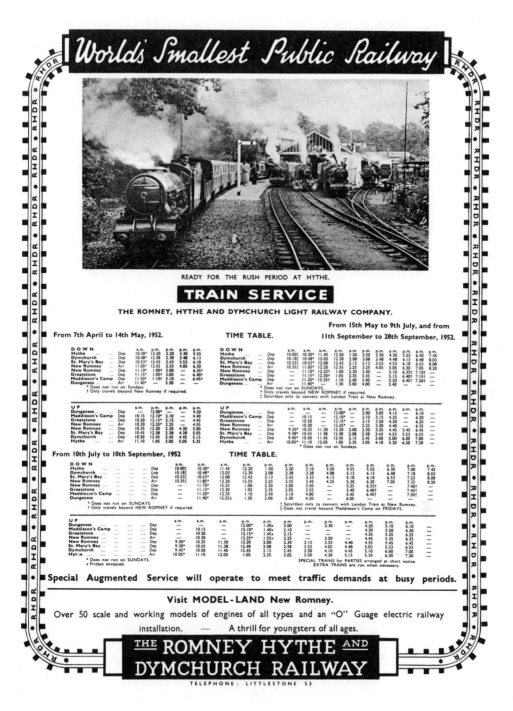

The original of this handsome advertising poster was photographically made and mounted on sturdy book board. The scene depicted is a commonplace on week-ends, when facilities of the line are taxed to capacity in providing service needed to haul the passengers on rides to the towns and resorts along the line.

This personal pride in all elements of railroading has paid off in an enviable safety record. The American practice of staggered rail joints gives a ride to the trains that is both smooth and quiet, for it demands a high standard of maintenance. If there is any depression at the joints, a sideways rocking motion is set up in the little train.

The grade crossings are without gates but on approaching them engineers are required to reduce speed to 5 m.p.h and give prolonged blasts on the whistle. Engineers stand well up on the footplate to obtain the best possible view of the highway. The vacuum brakes carried as standard equipment give them the greatest confidence. It is possible, in an emergency, to bring a train of sixteen cars to a dead stop from 25 m.p.h. in little more than its own length. Within the last few years only two accidents have occurred; and both of these are not without overtones of humor, even though tragedy was narrowly averted.

On August 11, 1952, the regular passenger train left Hythe station at 10:30 a.m., hauled by No. 10 *Doctor Syn*, restored to pristine glory after its sojourn in a bomb crater during World War II. On leaving Maddieson's Camp, the train encountered· a heavy thunder storm. The temporary engineer, Geoffrey Reddecliffe, stood up on the footplate to erect the canvas storm sheet used to protect the cab. But the bridges are low on this diminutive line and Engineer Reddecliffe, momentarily forgetful, was struck on the head by an overpass on the Dungeness side of the line. He was knocked insensible into the tender with the powerful little locomotive picking up speed.

A sixteen-year-old girl, Jane Turner, happened to be at the end window of the first car and saw the whole thing. After asking her companion to try to alert a man in the second car, she jumped for it and raced to the nearest telephone. Miraculously, she escaped injury. A breathless call was put in to Dungeness station.

Meanwhile, her companion finally succeeded in attracting the attention of the man in the next car. At great personal risk, he forced open the door in the tearing wind and climbed to the roof. Face down, he hauled himself along the two car roofs and into the tender of the runaway locomotive. He had never before set foot in the cab of a locomotive and the several levers, gauges and valves were a baffling array. But fortune smiled, for he grasped the most likely looking lever, which proved to be the throttle, and closed it.

Capt. Howey, alerted by Dungeness station, was already burning up the miles in his Jaguar and reached the stalled train in time to draw the fire from the locomotive's firebox, thus narrowly averting a boiler explosion. One of the most singular aspects of this incident was the fact that *Doctor Syn* had become partially derailed. The trailing wheels of the engine truck and the front pair of driving wheels were riding the ties, a providential fact that arrested progress once the throttle was closed. The hero of the wild ride was Leslie J. Ashman, who received the official congratulations of the line for a "very brave act."

Disaster was narrowly averted a few months later in the same general area. The section of single track from New Romney around the loop at Dungeness Lighthouse, traverses a wide, stony beach and is operated on the "staff and ticket" system. This system entails the use of a heavy metal key. The staff or key must be carried by the train on the loop and any other train waiting to enter the section cannot proceed without the engineer leaving the loop and handing the staff to the incoming engineer.

On the occasion in question, a special train had been despatched five minutes ahead of a regular train, rather like the pilot that precedes all Royal Trains in the standard gauges. In this case, the pilot was preparing the little road for a forthcoming non-stop run.

The engineer of the pilot was scheduled to go around the Dungeness loop and then wait at the mainline junction at what trainmen call Britannia Points. There, he could check out his staff with the Dungeness-bound train. He forgot to do this and steamed out onto the main line. His error hit him forcefully when he saw, bearing down on him under a fine head of steam, the express special he should have waited for.

Fortunately the other engineer took in the situation about the same instant. Each then set his brakes and jumped. The impact between the two locomotives—*Hurricane* and *Typhoon*— was not great and fortunately nobody was hurt. But the offending engineer, ruefully rubbing his bruises, made a mental resolve then and there to stick by regulations and never again let a hurricane get within striking distance of a typhoon.

The Romney, Hythe and Dymchurch Light Railway has always demonstrated a marked ability to sell itself to the British public. It is realized that the only way to meet rising costs is to attract more and more visitors, both from home areas and overseas and to offer each individual an experience it would be hard to match on any other miniature railroad. Most of the operating staff, especially the engineers, act like trained public relations officers. Their fine courtesy is not always repaid in kind; souvenir hunters stole the original bells from the Canadian-type locomotives and the headlight which once graced the No. 5 *Hercules;* and small boys too frequently carve their initials on the rolling stock.

But for the most part, passengers respond to the efforts of "The Friendly Line", as it is sometimes called, and come in increasing numbers to the Kentish shore, the big skies and the marsh with its bastions of ancient towns. It would seem that unless the sea encroaches once again on the marsh, the little Romney line will be with us forever.

© *J. C. Flemons*

Black Prince, No. 10, later re-named *Doctor Syn.* This engine and the No. 9, *Winston Churchill,* are built to Canadian Pacific Ry. standards and are the largest engines in the group. The bell on the pilot beam is far from following the shapliness of American locomotive bells and frames, more closely resembles the farm bells so common to America. All that is needed to complete the illusion of an American locomotive is a headlight, which British railroads never use.

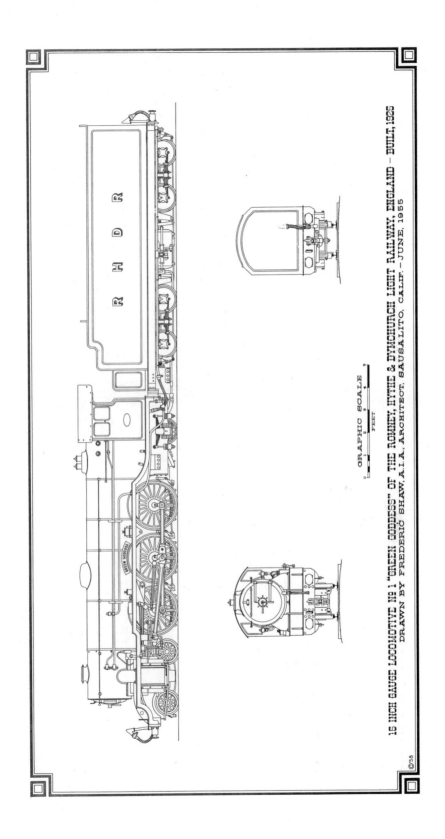

GRAPHIC SCALE

FEET

15 INCH GAUGE LOCOMOTIVE Nº 1 "GREEN GODDESS" OF THE ROMNEY, HYTHE & DYMCHURCH LIGHT RAILWAY, ENGLAND – BUILT, 1925
DRAWN BY FREDERIC SHAW, A.I.A., ARCHITECT, SAUSALITO, CALIF. – JUNE, 1955

©'58

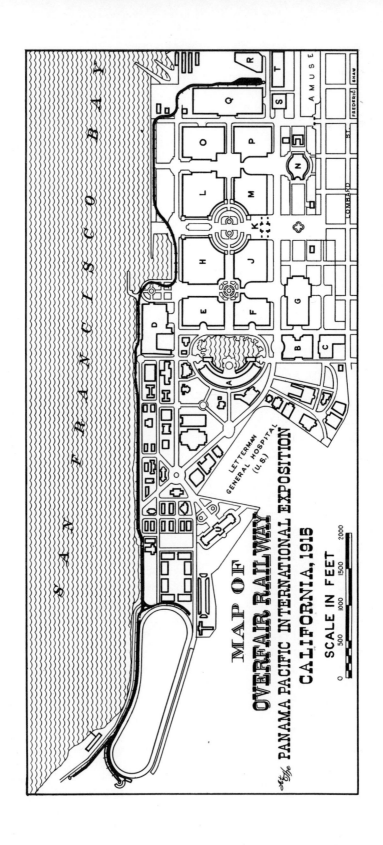

MAP OF
OVERFAIR RAILWAY
at the PANAMA PACIFIC INTERNATIONAL EXPOSITION
CALIFORNIA, 1915

SCALE IN FEET

0   500   1000   1500   2000

SAN FRANCISCO BAY

LETTERMAN GENERAL HOSPITAL (U.S.)

AMUSE

LOMBARD ST

FREDERIC SHAW

CHAPTER II

EXPOSITION PIKE

The Overfair Railway—Panama-Pacific-International Exposition

IN OCTOBER 1909, President Taft at a banquet at the Fairmont Hotel in San Francisco declared that the Panama Canal would be open to traffic in January 1915; and a mass meeting in the Merchants Exchange on December 7, 1909, ended in a resolve to organize an exhibition. Thus was the Panama-Pacific-International Exposition born, an idea keyed to the expansion of Pacific trade in which San Francisco would hold the Orient in fee like a Venice of the medieval world.

A young, mechanically-minded resident of the Bay Area was gripped by this concept of expanding world trade. His name was Louis M. MacDermot. Although still on the planning table, this exposition already linked in his own mind the arts and sciences and commerce of many nations. It was a small step to the thought of a transportation system which would physically link the international buildings. What would be better, he reasoned, than a miniature railway honoring the Twentieth Century's great Age of Steam? This was the heyday of the steam-hauled expresses on the main lines of the world. What could be more appropriate than a little steam-hauled excursion train girdling the world of the exposition grounds?

Nothing in the young man's early education and background had befitted him for such a scheme. Born to position and wealth, Louis MacDermot lived in Oakland, California, and the first person he discussed the idea with was an indulgent mother. It is entirely possible she was daunted by the magnitude of the project, but the favorite son must have over-ridden all objections, for it was soon under way with the securing of the franchise.

Since "Mac," as he was known, proposed to design and build all of the equipment for the Tom Thumb pike, the next step was a manufacturing plant. The palatial MacDermot home at 7th and Center Streets, Oakland, provided the location. A group of buildings was soon

19

Author's Collection

The handsome vertical engine seen here furnished all the power to operate the MacDermot machine shop. All parts, save boiler plates, which entered into fabrication of locomotives and cars for the Overfair Railway, were machined in this shop.

Author's Collection

Fabrication of cars for the 1915 exposition railroad required more space than was available on MacDermot's home premises. Consequently Mac leased a spacious warehouse nearby, in which sixty 16-seat passenger, five freight cars were built.

erected consisting of a spacious, well ventilated machine shop whose unobstructed clear span surmounted by a lantern shed ample daylight over the interior; and close by was a one-and-one-half story wood-frame building to act as a drafting room above and pattern shop below. Other smaller buildings of a temporary nature hovered close by. The machine tools of the plant were driven from a central overhead line shaft deriving its power from a handsome vertical steam engine.

"Mac's" first decision was the scale of his railroad equipment. He had undoubtedly studied a successful venture in Eastlake Park, Los Angeles, where John J. Cort, a Southern Pacific civil engineer had designed and built in the year 1905 a miniature railroad of 18-inch-gauge. Cort had also engineered the Ocean Park and Playa del Rey Railroad at nearby Venice, at a similar 18-inch-gauge. The two live steamers on this latter line, Prairie (2-6-2) type with eight-wheel tenders, were built to about one-third scale and could steam over the track at twenty miles per hour—equivalent to a mile-a-minute for their full-sized prototypes. Engineering—like art—is not born from a vacuum. What has gone before is important. MacDermot selected the one-third scale, but at a track gauge of nineteen inches.

"Mac" was a man of unusual mechanical skills, a neat, competent draftsman and versatile to an extreme in the use of machine tools. He made his drawings and handled his tools with the dedication of the perfectionist. With the shop buildings completed, machinery installed and drawings ready, "Mac" soon had mechanics busy and the Overfair Railway began to take shape.

The first design to leave the drawing board was for an 0-6-0T switching engine for use in the construction of the line at the Exposition grounds. Soon to follow were the passenger locomotives. In this regard, the young mechanical engineer had been thinking in terms of U. S. Class I railroads. It was not surprising, therefore, that the Oakland shops of the Overfair Railway soon rang to the fabrication of four of the most modern Pacific (4-6-2) locomotives. This type was the modern flyer of the day, and MacDermot demanded of himself exact miniatures for the Exposition.

The rolling stock was of little less consequence; nevertheless, the sixteen-seat passenger cars were constructed with the same painstaking care for detail. The car trucks, as they came from the assembly line in the shops, were sent to a nearby warehouse where a large crew of artisans finished the bodies and set them on the trucks. On this warehouse assembly line were also finished the freight cars which

Here, all the five locomotives were assembled. In the background stands L. M. MacDermot, builder of this unique 1/3-size steam railroad equipment. In the center is the completed No. 1913, the only one of the Pacifics on which Mac ever installed a bell.

This photo, made in 1914 at MacDermot's Oakland home shops, shows how all the line's locomotives and cars were transported on horse-drawn drays. Down to the Oakand ferry slip they went whence they were borne across San Francisco Bay to the Exposition ferry slip, hauled ashore and set on the line's rails.

were intended to serve a dual purpose. When the construction of the pike was completed and the Exposition a concourse of visitors from all over the world, the freight could snake through the grounds bearing the promotional messages of many household products. Advertising revenues from such a project could be enormous.

The boiler sheets for the locomotives were shaped in an Oakland commercial boiler works, the parts being assembled and riveted by the shop crews. Apart from this and the air pumps, everything used in the manufacture of motive power and rolling stock was made on the MacDermot estate.

The over-size air pumps aroused the curiosity of every beholder. They appeared so heavy as to threaten the balance of the locomotives. MacDermot had patterns almost completed for building his own air pumps to exact scale when a Westinghouse representative offered four 8-inch standard size pumps on a loan basis. Philosophically, it is the imperfection that arouses in us the keenest awareness and it may have been the imperfection of the over-sized air pumps that served to enhance the fitness of design of those miniatures.

Work proceeded according to schedule, interrupted only by the young engineer's tragic loss of his mother in the early fall of 1914 which called into question the whole problem of financing the ambitious project. Presumably, the legal counsellors of the estate realized how deeply committed the MacDermots were and that the best security for the heavy expenditures already made would be the successful operation of the pike when the Exposition opened the following year.

When the day did dawn for the opening of the Panama-Pacific-International Exposition, the Overfair Railway had built up a nice head of steam and was rarin' to go. From the southwest corner of the Machinery Palace, around the east side of that great structure to the Marina, curving around the Yacht Harbor and out to the Race Track and Polo Field, steamed the fair-girdling locomotives with their loaded passenger cars. The round trip was close to five miles. Two trains proved sufficient to handle the crowds on normal days, although a third train operated when special events attracted extra crowds. Although four Pacifics were built, only Nos. 1912, 1913 and 1914 were in actual operation. No. 1915 remained on the family's Oakland estate until MacDermot's death in 1948.

From the very beginning, the Overfair Railway was beset with difficulties. Our map discloses that the only track route the Exposition managers would approve merely skirted the northern edge of the

Author's Collection

Mac's favorite, the No. 1913. This photo shows MacDermot just after the locomotive was completed. In the background may be seen a portion of the machine shop and to the right the deckle-edged little building where all Mac's brain work took place, on his Oakland home grounds.

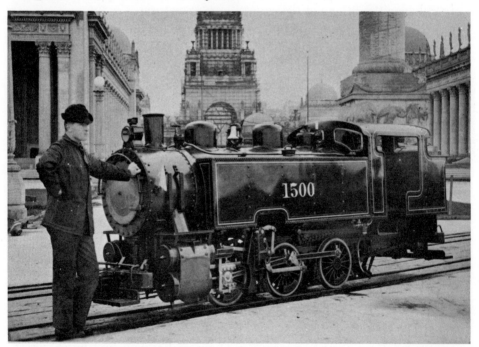

Robt: H. McFarland

Louis M. MacDermot standing by the handsome 19″ gauge switch engine he designed and built at his Oakland home. This was the first of the five he built for use on his Overfair Railway and was utilized in building the tracks on the Exposition grounds, where the photo was made.

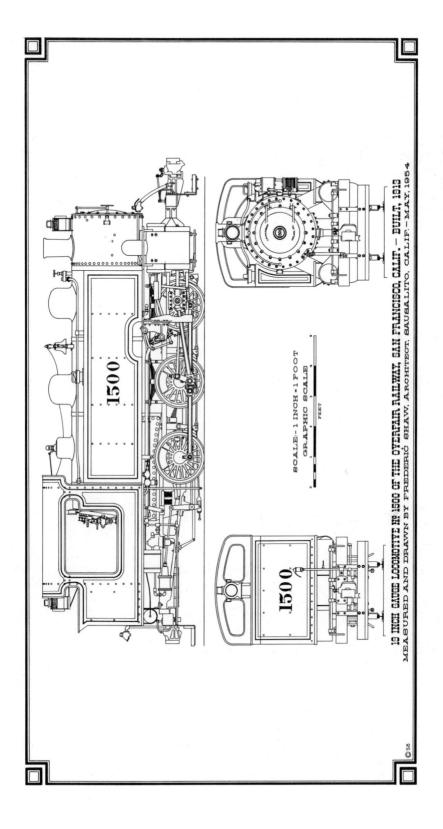

19 INCH GAUGE LOCOMOTIVE № 1500 OF THE OVERFAIR RAILWAY, SAN FRANCISCO, CALIF. — BUILT, 1913

MEASURED AND DRAWN BY FREDERIC SHAW, ARCHITECT, SAUSALITO, CALIF. — MAY, 1954

SCALE — 1 INCH = 1 FOOT

GRAPHIC SCALE

FEET

©56

A. Sheldon Pennoyer

Handsome mogul type (2-6-0) locomotive on the 18-inch gauge track at Eastlake Park, Los Angeles in 1901 as it crossed an arm of the lake. This fine locomotive later was bought by the street railway company of Portland, Oregon where it operated profitably in the park at Council Crest for many years. No record of its disposition exists.

Robt. H. McFarland

The Overfair Railway's 1912, 1913 and 1914 were the only Pacifics "Mac" used on the line. Normal daily operation called for use of but two trains, the third locomotive being a standby, used on days of unusually large crowds. The three locomotives were rotated to afford opportunities for maintenance.

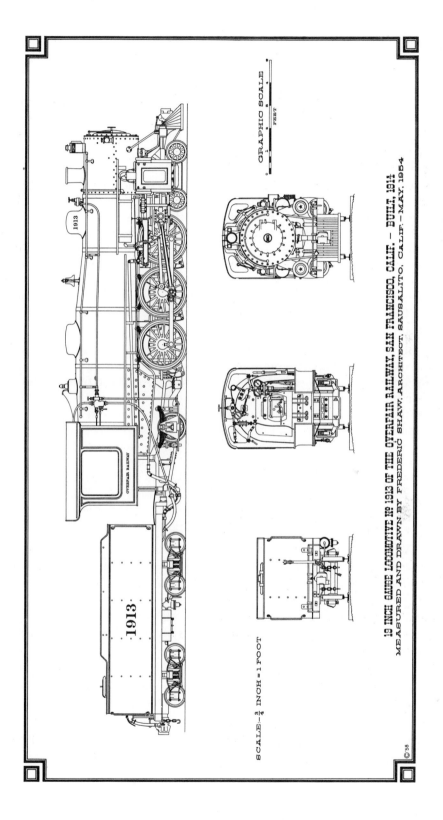

GRAPHIC SCALE

FEET

OVERFAIR RAILWAY

1913

1913

SCALE:- ¾ INCH = 1 FOOT

19 INCH GAUGE LOCOMOTIVE № 1913 OF THE OVERFAIR RAILWAY, SAN FRANCISCO, CALIF. — BUILT, 1914

MEASURED AND DRAWN BY FREDERIC SHAW, ARCHITECT, SAUSALITO, CALIF. — MAY, 1954

Ⓒ '56

grounds and provided little access to areas between palaces. Automotive equipment was operated by the Exposition management itself on the main avenues where most of the visitors moved, and purely for transportation purposes the Overfair Railway was much less convenient. On some special days, when extra large crowds were moving, the little pike was forbidden the right to operate at all!

Among the other slings and arrows of outrageous fortune was the short trestle over a minor arm of San Francisco Bay. MacDermot wanted to build this trestle to the scale of the trains. But the arbitrary decision was handed down that the trestle must be built, as an extra margin of safety, with the same size timbers required for a standard gauge railroad! The bridge cost twice as much as the original estimate. And what happened to the freight train whose advertising revenues could well have made the difference between profit and loss for the line? The fair management did not like that one either and denied it the right to operate.

But the worst display of arrogance and venality came when the great Panama-Pacific-International Exposition closed in November 1915. The little system of rails, built to match the concept of expanding Pacific trade, had to come up. Yet when the builder came to dismantle the buildings, the five miles of main line double track and sidings, the Exposition management claimed it all as leasehold improvements and not a penny was realized from this part of the tremendous investment. It was said that the little pike cost the MacDermot estate about $250,000, a sum barely matched by gross receipts from passenger fares. From these figures a mental balance sheet can be drawn. Mac, by way of explanation, bitterly complained of his "conductors' sticky fingers." He had never devised any method of checking them.

What happened to the Overfair rolling stock when the Exposition closed? MacDermot was no business tycoon; he took the arbitrary decisions of the Exposition management lying down, cut his losses, and herded his locomotives together in sheds on the Oakland family estate. The passenger cars were planted all over the yard without shelter of any kind. Thus the equipment remained for a full quarter century.

In 1939, MacDermot concluded an agreement with the Alameda Zoological Park at the southern end of the city of Oakland for a three-quarter mile loop of track. Pacific locomotive No. 1913, Mac's favorite, was reassembled and put to work hauling the old exposition cars loaded with children at a ten-cent fare. But the miniature live steamer was a mere shadow of its former self. The leading truck was gone, making her a dubious 0-6-2, and the boiler jacket was also non-existent. It was true that the curves on the little loop were too short for the truck to negotiate successfully, but the lack of the boiler jacket was itself an indication of a failing mind. MacDermot's eccentricities had grown with the passing years and cost him the loss of many friends. His conduct finally reached the point where the Zoo management had to sever all connections with the creator of the Overfair Railway and compel the removal of his equipment from the grounds.

Louis M. MacDermot died February 22, 1948, the beneficiary in his last months of a generous railroad engineer. It was not until his death that his friends learned about the disease which had affected his mind. Tragedy stalked him almost to the end.

Some people are remembered not only for what they have done but also for the things they dreamed of and somehow failed to do. MacDermot's place in the story of miniature railroads is secure. He was of average stature, about five feet eight inches tall, slight and never weighing over one hundred thirty-five pounds. His blond hair was prematurely gray, yet his face gathered few lines with the passing years. Given neither to great enthusiasms nor outbursts of anger, his movements were deliberate and precise. To watch his sensitive fingers handle his drawings or an artifact of his own creation was to understand one facet of this self-contained man whose speech never revealed his other attainments. His powers of conversation were limited when discussing generalities, but when discoursing about things mechanical and trying to focus plans and aspirations for future use of his locomotives and cars, he came alive.

Something happened in his later life between the concept and the realization, as it does to many of us. The loop line he built in Alameda Zoological Gardens never really came to anything but a token accomplishment. At one time he envisioned re-laying the whole line of track on the 78-mile right-of-way of the former narrow gauge North Pacific Coast from Point Reyes to Monte Rio in California. He wanted to acquire title to the track and right-of-way and move one rail over from the narrow gauge of three feet to suit his own equipment at a gauge of nineteen inches. He talked at the time of that old road's abandonment, of picnic trains with nurses to shepherd the children for a day's outing; of piggyback, light trucks to go into the hinterland served by the railroad to pick up and haul to the stations farm products in special containers, there to be transferred to specially designed flatbed cars for another rail haul to a central distribution point. The president of

Here stands locomotive No. 1914 and its train at the eastern end of the Overfair Railway at Machinery Hall. It will soon back out onto the wye and start its journey to the western, race-track end of the line.

the recently abandoned North Pacific Coast has disclosed that had MacDermot made such an offer, the project could easily have been consummated.

The Fates, which had dealt roughly with MacDermot during his lifetime, finally relented when the equipment came up for sale. It fell into the hands of a retired locomotive engineer, Mr. Billy Jones, of Los Gatos, California, for the sum of $5,200. Few other people would have paid more than the price of junk.

Mr. Jones saw in those steam engines a chance to preserve for others some outstanding examples of miniature motive power. They have been reassembled and restored to the condition of their Exposition days. Converted to oil burners and mechanical lubricators, they are maintained in trust for all railroad enthusiasts. Mr. Jones operates his own 18-inch-gauge loop of track with a miniature live steamer which belonged originally to the Ocean Park and Playa del Rey Railroad at Venice, California. MacDermot must have studied this Venice line before his Overfair Railway reached the drawing board.

So the little Overfair Pacifics remain in good company, waiting their chance to steam once more. And in this buccolic atmosphere the spirit of "Mac" finds rest and contentment, as a never-ending stream of visitors, seeing his engines, live again the Exposition days of 1915.

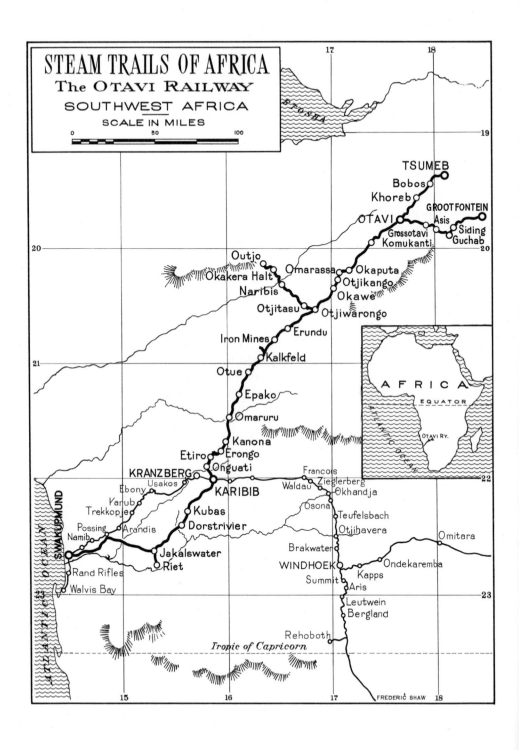

STEAM TRAILS OF AFRICA
The OTAVI RAILWAY
SOUTHWEST AFRICA
SCALE IN MILES
0   50   100

ETOSHA

TSUMEB
Bobos
Khorab
OTAVI   GROOTFONTEIN
                         Asis
Grossotavi   Siding
Komukanti   Guchab

Outjo
Okakera Halt   Omarassa   Okaputa
Naribis   Otjikango
                           Okawe
Otjitasu   Otjiwarongo
                  Erundu
Iron Mines
        Kalkfeld
Otue
        Epako
    Omaruru
        Kanona
Etiro   Erongo
     Ohguati
KRANZBERG   Francois
        Usakos   Zieglerberg
Ebony   Waldau   Okhandja
Karub   Osona
Trekkopje   KARIBIB
Possing Arandis   Kubas   Teufelsbach
Namib   Dorstrivier   Otjihavera
                                          Omitara
Rand Rifles   Jakalswater   Brakwater
              Riet   WINDHOEK   Ondekaremba
Walvis Bay   Summit   Kapps
                                    Aris
                            Leutwein
                            Bergland
                    Rehoboth
        Tropic of Capricorn

SWAKOPMUND

ATLANTIC OCEAN

AFRICA
EQUATOR
OTAVI RY.

FREDERIC SHAW

CHAPTER III

STEAM TRAILS OF AFRICA

The Otavi Mining and Railway Company

IT IS IMPOSSIBLE for anyone not familiar with the territory of South-West Africa to visualize the vastness and the enormity of sparsely settled areas, the tiny settlements designated as towns which are threaded by the longest two-foot gauge railway in the world, the Otavi Mining and Railway Company. It was pioneered in the teeth of almost every adversity man and nature could provide—war, native uprisings, drought, locust hordes, floods and tenuous communications. Its story forges one of the most important links in the history of the narrow gauge.

Initially, it was a British enterprise, for the South-West Africa Company was formed in London in 1892, capitalized at 300,000 pounds, and was granted a concession by the German Government which included exclusive mineral rights over an area of 22,000 square miles and the already known copper deposits of Otavi. Surveys were made for a railroad from the coast at Swakopmund to Windhuk, a distance of 238 miles, and to Tsumeb, 354 miles. According to Lord Lugard's book, *The Dual Mandate in British Tropical Africa,* experience with the Festiniog Railway had insured the adoption of the policy that development in certain areas of Africa should never take place with slow, broad or standard gauge lines involving a big load of debt. Rather, it should be accomplished by cheap, quickly built narrow-gauge light railways with lateral feeder roads, not lateral feeder branch lines. And a Mr. Angus, who made the survey, undoubtedly had this in mind.

But in 1898 a convention was called at which the German Government withdrew the exclusive rights to railway construction from the South-West Africa Company. All plans and surveys prepared for the company, so far as they related to a proposed Swakopmund-Windhuk railroad, were handed over free of charge to the German authorities. Other mining rights were granted as compensation and the amended

Construction gang in cut circa 1906. The Otavi from the beginning was plagued with labor troubles and native uprisings due to repressive colonial policies.

Engine No. 154 at Usakos. Little is known of this locomotive save for the fact that originally there were ten of these odd looking side tanks ordered from Arnold Jung. They may well have been the first Otavi motive power.

agreement in no way prohibited the company from constructing a railroad, but it did break their monopoly.

This Swakopmund-Windhuk railroad was already under construction by the German military authorities. All material had to be landed through the surf. When Swakopmund was founded, a mole was built to form protection for small craft, but two months after its official opening, sand carried north by the ocean currents had formed a bar from its end to the shore, over which it was possible to walk dry shod at low tide. The formidable difficulties of supply notwithstanding, the 60 centimeter road (23.62 inches) to Windhuk was completed in five years.

Meanwhile the South-West Africa Company was pushing ahead with its plans for a railroad to Tsumeb. Thirty men were sent out from England in 1900 to the site of the copper deposits, and at the same time an expeditionary force of railway experts under T. Toennesen reached the hinterland. Reports made to London headquarters repeatedly emphasized the fact that transportation was by far the most critical problem between Swakopmund and the proposed mines at Otavi and Tsumeb. The area was the most sterile to be found south of the Sahara.

At first it was planned to build a standard gauge line from Port Alexander in Portugese West Africa southeast up the Muende River valley and via Etoscha Pan·to the Tsumeb with the thought in mind that at a later date it could be extended to Rhodesia to form a trans-African railway, a traverse line comparable to the dream of Cecil Rhodes for a Cape to Cairo railway. But the plan, of course, conflicted with the basic British policies of railroads in under-developed countries.

In an effort to find a satisfactory solution, the problem was referred to Arthur Koppel & Company of Berlin. The Koppel Company sent out its own survey party and recommended the 60 centimeter gauge, based on the belief that it would meet all traffic requirements for many years to come, its initial cost would be within reason and it could be built in much less time than a standard gauge line. That Koppel was influenced in his recommendations by the fundamental of British railway policy for under-developed countries cannot be doubted.

There was some question as to whether the line should be built only between Tsumeb and Karibib, using the State Northern Railroad from Karibib to the coast, but it was strongly recommended that an entirely independent line be built the whole way, as the government imposed restricted axle loads.

Steam rail motor car No. 1. Accommodations were two compartments for Europeans and four for natives; and this compact rail unit also included a mail compartment, a sizable coal bunker and an engine room.

Robert Louis Stevenson's phrase about "hills tawny as a lion and clothed only in the blue transparent air" comes to mind as one looks on this picture of Khan River station on the Otavi Mining and Railway Company.

While plans for the railroad were being discussed, the entire project was sold to the Otavi Mining and Railway Company, an all-German organization formed in 1900, for 55% of the interest in that firm. Although active control of the Otavi Company, as it was generally called, passed over to the owners of the South-West Africa Company, the increased financial standing brought about by the merger, insured sufficient capital to finance the undertaking. The new company, for it was practically that, had a fully paid up capital stock of 1,000,000 pounds. In exchange for the 55% interest, the South-West Africa Company turned over to the Otavi organization 1,000 square miles of mining rights therein, plus all rights to construct and operate the proposed railroad. Thus, although the South-West Africa Company retained its corporate identity, it stepped out of the immediate German South-West Africa picture, for it owned no other interests in the territory at that time.

In 1903 a ship loaded with materials was sent to Africa and the grade was begun at Swakopmund. The final survey was run from there to Otavi, approximately 300 miles to the northeast, and a preliminary survey completed to Tsumeb. Advantage was occasionally taken of the natural depressions and dry gullies, irrespective of the fact that some of the latter were subject to flash floods. This ignorance of local conditions on the part of locating engineers accounted later for many of the washouts along the route.

The first sod was hardly turned before a serious native uprising complicated matters. Herero natives had been recruited in large numbers to do the grading; and at the first signs of real trouble, which had been brewing a long time on account of the repressive German policies, the majority returned to their villages to take up arms. Since the Hottentots had already revolted and the native labor situation was completely out of hand, the Otavi turned to Europe and imported 300 Italians. As it turned out, the native uprisings benefitted the 2-foot gauge road: the Italians were in a position to dictate terms and struck for higher wages; and the German military authorities, in order to contain the native uprisings and strike at the enemy's stronghold in the hinterland, promised the little railway a bonus based on the number of days under the estimated time it would have taken the builders to reach Omaruru.

As the stakes were high, the railroad hired an additional 750 Italians and 500 Ovambo natives. But the newly arrived Italians soon learned the bad habits of their compatriots, and although the Ovambos continued working, strike followed strike and the grading and laying of rails proceeded at the clogged pace of the dreamer.

In the spring of 1905 conditions took a turn for the better. The Italians gradually speeded up their work, spurred on partly by additional bonuses but mainly by the increasing availability of competitive labor. Hereros began to straggle in and surrender to the authorities rather than starve to death in the desert. As they surrendered they were given the choice of working on the railroad or confinement in compounds. Many chose to work on the railroad, although their lot was little better than that of the natives confined. Many died from brutal treatment, disease and hunger before they were released from their "voluntary" servitude. Food and a heavy rod made workmen out of the unfortunate Hereros and it became painfully evident to the European contingent that the contractors could easily do without them.

The African country traversed is just as inhospitable now as it was then. The first 140 miles of the Otavi run through the furnace heat of a terrible desert and wide stretches of scrub-covered country broken with kopjes. Extensive bridging was found necessary to carry the track across gullies and rivulets, there being in all 110 of these structures built of steel, the deckplate girder type being generally used.

Some idea of the extent of the delay caused by strikes and insurrection may be gathered from the fact that although 23 months were required to construct the line from Swakopmund to Omaruru, 145 miles, the second section, from Omaruru, 215 miles, required but another year.

Water was one of the worst problems confronting the little railway, transcending labor troubles and veld fires started by the Hereros. On the first section every pint of water for drinking purposes had to be brought up from the coast. As the end-of-steel advanced, the difficulties increased. A German water-diviner used his rod with scant success. When Usakos was reached the situation was eased somewhat by a local discovery; but the water had to be softened before it could be used by the engines. Accordingly, a water softening plant had to be brought up country and erected. This, however, was useless for domestic purposes, and when the line pushed on beyond Omaruru special water trains were run for the convenience of the workmen.

It is unfortunate that records of the equipment used during the early construction days no longer exist. According to the records of Arthur Koppel & Co., that firm furnished all the locomotives under the contract covering the construction and outfitting of the little railway for the Otavi Mining and Railway Company. Subsequent catalogues issued by Koppel showed some of these engines, all with Koppel builder's plates, but it is an established fact that the majority of the engines furnished were built by other firms. Such illustrations were made possible by retouching photographs supplied by the builders. There is an indication that Koppel furnished new or second-hand motive power to be used to haul construction trains until locomotives ordered from sub-contractors could be delivered. There is no actual proof that such was the case, but the lapsed time between the actual beginning of construction and the arrival of the first known lot of new engines indicates this to have been so. It is known that a small engine with a sunflower stack and a 4-wheel tender was in service at an early date. It may be supposed that she was the, or one of the, engines used to haul construction trains.

A year after the last section of the Otavi was officially completed and turned over to the owners, the South-West Africa Company again entered the picture. In 1907 the Company opened mines around Groot-fontein and built a railroad southwest to Otavi, 56¼ miles, and entered into an agreement whereby the Otavi Company operated and main-tained the branch. The line was completed in 1908; and soon after this the government purchased both the Otavi Company's railroad and the Grootfontein-Otavi line for a total of 22,000,000 marks ($5,236,-000), immediately leasing both lines back to the Otavi Mining and Railway Company under terms of a 30-year lease.

The peak of expansion and operation under German ownership was reached just prior to the outbreak of World War I in 1914. The mining industry had expanded steadily and the little railway had kept pace with it, bringing in heavier equipment and improving the service. The time table put into effect on January 1, 1913, scheduled the opera-tion of 47 trains each week: 4 express trains, 14 mixed trains and 29 freight trains. Regular express and mixed trains provided accommoda-tions for first and second class passengers, a car for natives and one for baggage and express. Mixed and freight trains stopped as required to take on or discharge passengers at points outside the prescribed station locations. Express trains were prohibited from so doing unless it was for pre-arranged pickups of perishable or fragile items.

The tides of war rolled over the Otavi on January 14, 1915 when Union of South Africa forces under Colonel Skinner marched into a deserted Swakopmund. The entire population had moved out on the heels of the German Army, which, realizing it was in an excellent posi-

Otavi freight-train crossing the Khan River. Although one of the most waterless narrow gauge railways in the world, the Otavi suffered disasterous floods on occasions. The Khan River flooded in 1925 halting traffic for several weeks. Note ant hill in foreground.

tion to be cut off from the interior, had retreated to the East in the general direction of Karibib. As they retreated they completely stripped the Otavi as far as Rossing, 30 miles from Swakopmund and the abandoned but still intact State Northern Railway to a point 14½ miles beyond Rossing; and it was the logistical problem of the Union forces in pursuit of the Germans that occasioned the rebuilding of the Otavi to South African "standard" gauge. But the famous Boer, General Botha, moved too fast for the widening of the track gauge to 42 inches. It was decided to discontinue conversion of the Otavi at Ebony, ten miles short of Usakos. Although skilled in demolition and mining the little railway, the retreating German Army had reckoned without the German population. Generally, they disagreed with their government's native policy; and apart from the port of Swakopmund itself, had welcomed the invading Boers as the lesser of two evils. Some of them lent active support to the rehabilitation of the line, revealing where equipment was hidden. At war's end, 14½ kilometers of track suddenly reappeared with the German engineers and workmen responsible for removing it, and for one day, they assisted in replacing it.

Broadening of the little railway to the standard 42 inches between Ebony and Usakos, 35 miles, was begun immediately after the cessation of hostilities and completed as far as Usakos. But Usakos was not a suitable southern terminal for the narrow gauge; and after August 1, 1915, when the military released the railways of the territory to a commission headed by a Director of Railways, it was moved to Karibib where the necessary facilities for gauge-to-gauge transhipment were available.

Nobody who has traveled desert railways the world over would be under any illusion that trips north from Karibib on the Otavi were any better. Strabo wrote of the oriental town of Susa that when a lizard attempted to cross the noon-day street it was baked at half the distance! The Otavi was not quite in the same category, but the usual discomforts of dust, heat and flies made the long haul to the terminal at Tsumeb a test of endurance. Food was a problem for the individual, who had a choice of bringing enough to last for the trip or relying on the hotels in the larger villages where the train stopped. Train schedules were arranged to allow sufficient time for passengers to eat; but a late train arrival, which was the rule rather than the exception, cut into the layover time and placed a strain on the passenger's digestion.

To alleviate this situation, a standard coach was converted to a dining car and entered the Otavi service on August 4, 1916. It was not

The Executive Car built by Waggonfabrik Gebruder Hofman & Co., Breslau, Germany. Businessmen on the long haul north from Karibib could enjoy office facilities, a bathroom and a kitchen. The office was converted to a bedroom at night.

Motor Trolley *Crown Prince*. This trolley was constructed specially for the projected visit of German Crown Prince Wilhelm in 1914. It once attained a speed of 86 MPH and was powered by a six-cylinder Daimler-Benz gasoline engine.

only a financial success but proved popular with everyone save the hotel owners along the route. So far as known, this was the only 2-foot gauge dining car ever operated.

With the fluctuations of the mining of copper ore came steadily increasing passenger business. Improved service was offered by increasing the speed of certain trains, cutting the running time between Usakos and Tsumeb in half, the journey in either direction taking one day instead of two. The fast schedules became effective June 9, 1924 and were made possible by the introduction of vacuum-braked rolling stock. Three fast trains were scheduled in both directions each week. Slower trains continued to be made up of hand-braked rolling stock.

The summer of 1924 was made notable by the invasion of locusts. Frequently trains were stalled on rails effectively greased by the squashed bodies of the pests; and in efforts to keep the track clear, an engine was fitted with a steam spraying apparatus which proved most effective. The next year the worst floods in forty years engulfed sections of the road. Riding the Otavi was nothing if not eventful and it was not surprising that persons who had to make a trip into the interior sometimes preferred to take a chance of getting his automobile stuck in the sand rather than risk flood, drought or locusts. The slow decrease of passenger business resulted in the discontinuance of dining car service in 1931. The cars were converted into trainmen's cabooses. But as human patronage fell off, more and more dairy products moved over the narrow gauge. Ventilated cars for the conveyance of cream proved unsuitable and cars with coke-lined bodies substituted. During July and August, 1933, the first commercial crop of grapefruit shipped from the territory moved by water-cooled trucks from Otavi. It in no way benefitted the narrow gauge but held out a promise of new business if the highway transportation proved unsatisfactory.

The period 1933 to 1936 when the copper mines at Tsumeb were closed was a difficult one for the little Otavi. The bottom fell out of the freight business. And many of the Road Motor Service feeder routes out of Otjiwarongo, the feeder routes envisioned in the original concept of narrow gauge railways in under-developed countries, were abandoned. But with the reopening of the Tsumeb mines in 1936 due to German interest in strategic war materials, freight traffic again picked up. Twenty Germans arrived to take over supervisory positions, bringing the New Order as taught and practised in the Third Reich. When war was declared in Europe in 1939 the Union of South Africa, although technically at war with Germany, had to take account of anti-British sentiment and allowed the Germans to operate the mines

A class HB Henschel No. 63 of 0-6-2 type. For long hauls across desert country tenders were found essential and the HB's were eventually replaced in 1911 by heavy power 2-8-2 superheated engines with double truck tenders.

Machine shop and partly constructed water tank at Karibib. After 1915 Karibib was the southern terminal for the little Otavi.

for a while. But in September, 1940, the German personnel were moved to concentration camps for safe keeping and the Tsumeb mines were closed down again.

The economic sun rose again on the little Otavi when in 1946 the Tsumeb mine was sold for 1,010,000 pounds to the Tsumeb Corporation, Ltd. This corporation was owned by the Newmont Mining Corporation and the American Metal Company Ltd., of New York who owned the controlling interest, Selection Trust Ltd., British South Africa Company of London, Union Corporation Ltd., South West Africa Company and O'okiep Copper Company of South Africa. The new company concentrated initially on the export of lead ore. The little mining town of Tsumeb began to grow overnight into one of the largest and most modern cities of the territory. From 1947 to 1952, 400 new homes were built. These were almost bonanza years and the general economic picture has continued to improve to the present day.

As has already been noted, records of the motive power are incomplete. The first consignment of locomotives of which we have record was delivered by Arn. Jung of Jungenthal, Germany, and consisted of ten 0-6-2 side tanks. A second order of five identical engines was placed before delivery of the original order. These engines weighed 48,880 lbs. and their cylinders were 11.81″ in diameter. They had 27.56″ drivers, 21.65″ truck wheels, 484 sq. ft. of heating surface and 176 p.s.i. boiler pressure. The tractive effort was 6,000 lbs. Another order was placed at approximately the same time with Henschel & Sohn for ten engines of basically the same design. Three fast passenger locomotives were supplied by Henschel in 1905. The following year, two further Henschels of 0-6-2 type were delivered; and after 1907 no additional engines of that type were ordered. Henschel supplied instead three 0-6-0 units.

For the long hauls auxiliary tenders had proved essential and 20 large double-truck units went into service after 1907. They had a water capacity of 2,200 gallons and a fuel capacity of 7,700 lbs. It is a noteworthy operating detail that coal was transferred from the tender by a native riding there. He shoveled coal into a chute built into the rear wall of the engine cab, by which it was deposited in a pile on the cab deck within easy reach of the fireman. For boiler feed each engine was equipped with two injectors and a duplex pump. Prior to the delivery of the tenders, additional feedwater was hauled in oblong tanks mounted on flat cars.

The complete story of the little Otavi's stable of iron horses would fill a volume in itself. The first really heavy power was completed in

Paul Darrell Collection

Beyer-Peacock & Co. Garratt type 2-6-2 + 2-6-2 locomotive. Two were built for the Otavi Rwy. There are over three dozen of these 2-foot gauge Garratt type locomotives now in service in Africa, each capable of hauling over 180 tons over the most adverse grades and curvature and doing it with substantially greater economy than the non-articulated type locomotive.

H. T. Crittenden Collection

Tsumeb Station Yard. After 1946 the little mining town of Tsumeb started to grow into one of the largest and most modern cities of the territory.

1911 by Henschel with three 2-8-2 superheated engines with large 8-wheel tenders. They had 15.8" diameter cylinders with a 17.7" stroke. The drivers were 33.86" diameter, the truck wheels 21.65" diameter. The heating surface was 901 sq. ft. with the superheater increasing that figure by 244.3 sq. ft. Weight was approximately 132,000 lbs. with a tractive effort of 13,660 lbs.

Just prior to the outbreak of World War I, Henschel completed for the Company two exceptionally fine Pacific engines, numbered 31 and 32. Although the builder's records indicate actual delivery, the engines were not among those turned over to the A.A.E.C. at the surrender in 1915. They vanished into the limbo of the burning desert.

Motive power was divided into six classifications. The Jungs were always simply designated as "Jungs", while the small 0-6-2 Henschels numbered in the 20's were officially Class HA. The larger Henschel 0-6-2's, numbered in the 50's and 60's, were Class HB, the 0-6-0's were Class HC, the 40's Class HD and the missing Pacifics Class HE. From June, 1915 onwards, 14 engines were supplied from the South African Railways. They were a mixed assortment of American Baldwins and British built locomotives. In 1922, six new Class D 2-8-2 Henschels were delivered. The engines were excellent machines, although flange wear was excessive owing to the rigid nature of the wheel base for some sections of the winding Otavi.

In an effort to increase the tonnage per train, a Class NGG12 Garratt locomotive No. 56, built by the Franco-Belge Company, was transferred to South West Africa in 1927. She proved such a success that two more were sent up from the Union, No. 50 in September 1928, and No. 49 a month later. They were returned in 1933.

The records of Otavi motive power would not be complete without reference to the rail motor coach constructed specially for Crown Prince Wilhelm's visit in 1914. Much was made of this event, but of course war intervened and Prince Wilhelm never came. Known as *Crown Prince,* the coach attained a speed of 87 m.p.h. on its trial run in June, 1914, and earned for itself the title of the fastest narrow-gauge rail car in the world. The power plant of this 14,740 lb. speedster was a six-cylinder Daimler-Benz gasoline engine.

During the early war years it completely disappeared. It was discovered by accident in 1916 when a yardman at Usakos noticed two small boys using an isolated shed. The yardman, his curiosity aroused, levered back a loose board when the boys were absent — and found the *Crown Prince* inside! It was checked over thoroughly and put back to work as an inspection trolley.

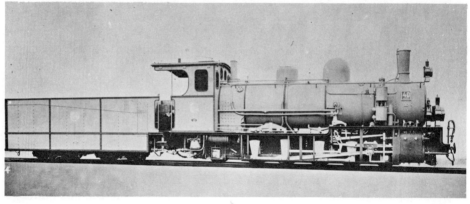

A class HD Henschel. These 2-8-2 locomotives were reportedly the most successful motive power on the little Otavi.

Freight train crossing one of the deckplate girder bridges on the Otavi. In the
first 140 miles of track there are no fewer than 110 of these structures.

The fact that the road was built primarily to handle ore required that the majority of the freight cars be for that purpose. The initial consignment consisted of several types, however. All cars were double-trucked and equipped with self-acting brakes working on all four wheels of one truck, actuated by a brakeman on each car. As regards the other rolling stock of the little Otavi, no thought had been given to passenger service at the time the line was projected. Three passenger cars were placed on order in 1906 when the passenger business potential was realized. Prior to their actual delivery, in 1907, passengers were hauled in cars fitted with benches and canvas awnings.

The new stock was of the double truck, open-platform type, divided into two compartments for first and second-class passengers. Winds of hurricane force were an added hazard of the Otavi; and to keep the passenger cars on the rails, the space between the channels of the underframe was filled with reinforced concrete, thus substantially lowering the center of gravity. Traveling this little railway was nothing if not adventurous.

Another type of car which deserves mention was the Business Car, which we in the United States would surely have called an Executive Car. It was a 24,200 lb. double-truck compartment coach consisting of an office (convertible into a bedroom), a bathroom and a kitchen. Four new sleeping cars were added in 1938. The catalogue of motive power and rolling stock is seemingly endless. Over fifty years of operation and over two hundred miles of track, washed over by violent natural forces and all the perils the human spirit is heir to, the little Otavi endured, thereby achieving for itself a unique place in the annals of the 60 cm. gauge.

At the time of writing, over 2,000 tons of copper ore are are being railed down weekly from the Tsumeb mines and the railroad administration has already made plans for the broadening of the little Otavi to the standard South African gauge of 42 inches. Work is to take three years. So the twilight of the live steamers of the African narrow gauge will, in the not too distant future, fade into night.

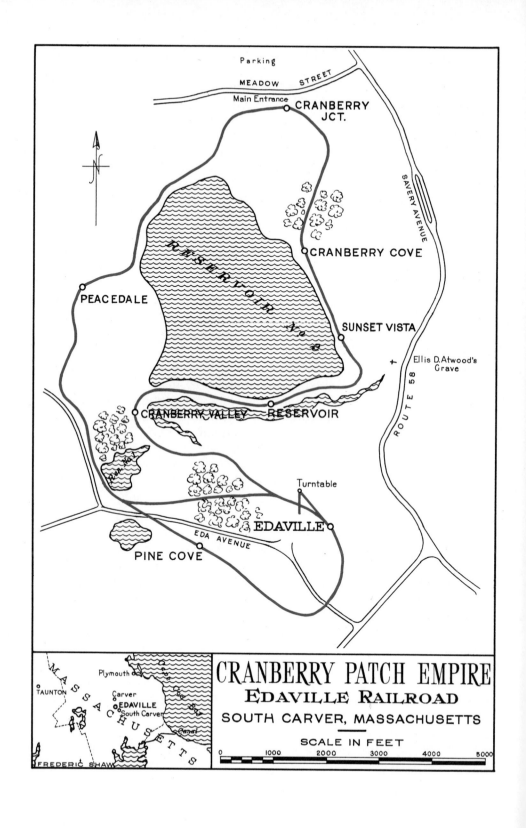

CRANBERRY PATCH EMPIRE
EDAVILLE RAILROAD
SOUTH CARVER, MASSACHUSETTS

SCALE IN FEET

CHAPTER IV

CRANBERRY PATCH EMPIRE

The Edaville Railroad

THE EFFORTS OF two men have brought into being one of the greatest miniature railroad shows on earth, the Edaville Railroad at South Carver, Massachusetts. The man who conceived the project was Ellis D. Atwood who operated one of the most productive cranberry bogs in the country at the same location; and the railroadian who followed in the footsteps of the founder is F. Nelson Blount of Warren, Rhode Island, author, with Fred Richardson, of a book entitled "Along the Iron Trail" and a great collector of railroadiana.

The Edaville Railroad was originally the offshoot of the old "two-foot empire" of Maine, a system of over two hundred miles of narrow-gauge which thrived in the Victorian era in the New England woods and outlived its economic usefulness long before the last of the lines was demolished in 1941.

The "two-foot empire" actually started only a few miles from South Carver—at Billerica, Massachusetts. The "empire builder" was a Bostonian, George E. Mansfield. Mansfield had been in Britain and taken a trip on the Festiniog Railway in Wales, a 23.5-inch-gauge mountain line which is acknowledged to be the precursor of the world's miniature roads. It had been demonstrated to him that such a gauge was not only perfectly safe but also presented many features to make it an attractive economic proposition for a certain type of terrain. The Billerica and Bedford RR, which Mansfield promoted in 1879, was America's first two-foot-gauge railroad.

Mansfield followed this first venture with an excursion into the Maine woods, and the formation of the Sandy River RR as a result. He also organized, in 1881, the Bridgton and Saco River RR. These were but three independent roads of a two-foot network, threading lumber towns and lake resorts, suffering mergers and never economically too stable. One of the roads, the Sandy River and Rangeley Lakes RR, lasted until 1935. Another, the Bridgton and Harrison RR lasted until 1941. It was the demolition of the track and equipment

E. G. Handy

The handsome parlor car RANGELEY originally built by the famed Jackson & Sharp Co. of Wilmington, Delaware in 1901 for the Sandy River & Rangeley Lakes Railroad of Maine, was "the most expensive passenger unit" ever owned by the company. It seated 26 passengers in its three compartments. This car now rides the iron of the Edaville Railroad and is that road's most prized possession.

Edaville Museum

Interior of the world's only two-foot-gauge parlor car RANGELEY which once rolled over the rails of the Sandy River & Rangeley Lakes up in Maine. These rotating chairs look so comfortable one would probably not mind the roll and sway of this diminutive car.

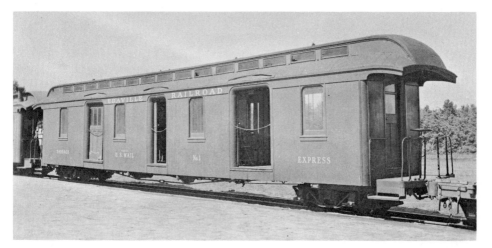

R. C. Gray

Typical of the diminutive passenger train rolling stock is this baggage-mail-express car, ex-Bridgton & Harrison of Maine. Age has brought on the "sway-back" so common to all ancient wooden cars.

The Dicksons

Curator and Mrs. Burton Logan of the Edaville Museum, South Carver, Mass. Mr. Logan has one of the largest collections of ancient toy trains in the United States, gathered over many years. There is insufficient room in this part of the museum to display all Mr. Logan's collection, so the items are rotated from time to time.

of these two roads that inspired Ellis D. Atwood to enter a race with the junkman. He managed to buy some of the usable track and units of the motive power and rolling stock.

Mr. Atwood's cranberry bog needed a utility line, and an idea had been taking shape in his mind for some time that he could combine a functional railway with a reliquary of the "two-foot empire." He did his own engineering on the line and turned his cranberry crews loose when he could spare them for extracurricular duties such as track layers and train crews. Work proceeded at such a rapid rate that in 1948 the physical properties of the Edaville Railroad were 5.5 miles of main line; 0.6 miles of cutoff; and 1 mile of yard, making a grand total of 7.1 miles. Apart from the bog engines, motive power included:

> No. 3 0-4-4T Vulcan, ex Monson RR No. 3
> No. 4 0-4-4T Vulcan, ex Monson RR No. 4
> No. 7 2-4-4T Baldwin, ex Bridgton & Saco River No. 7
> No. 8 2-4-4T Baldwin, ex Bridgton & Saco River No. 8

Included in the rolling stock was the "Pondicherry," a Bridgton car built by Laconia Car Works seventy years ago or more; a sister car, the "Mount Pleasant"; a coach with double windows and stained glass named "Elthea" in honor of Mrs. Atwood; and the Sandy River parlor car "Rangeley."

The "Rangeley" is a real period piece. The car rides smoothly on the 56-pound rail but it does seem a bit narrow, having but one swivel chair on each side of the aisle. Amenities include a toilet and car heater. At the far end is the smoking section—two leather seats and a couple of chairs. To slip into a brown study is the easiest thing in the world in such an atmosphere: one can imagine the old "empire" passengers, the ladies in crinoline gowns and Victorian coiffures, the men snipping the ends of their cigars with tiny gold scissors and the boys in Buster Brown collars. Today, those inlaid woods, the filigree designs on the ceiling, the brass lamps and expensive green leather upholstery would cost a king's ransom. Despite bantam size, these cars denote a greater amplitude of life, a more leisurely existence.

It is easy to get sentimental about life as it was lived on those old two-footers. Freight and passenger business was always uncertain. Climatic conditions were severe. In 1884 a passenger train was three days covering the eighteen miles from Farmington to Phillips due to huge snow drifts. Each trip was something of an adventure. The incidence of derailments, collisions, snow slides, floods, drought and forest fires was extremely high. Life, in fact, was raw. But it was a

good life as well. Engine crews maintained in their lockers shot guns
or rifles for the deer that abounded. What engine crew today would
not take pleasure in such opportunities for sporting diversion? But
raw or leisurely, the life of the "empire" has come down to the Edaville visitor in these little cars and can be soaked up even in the
bustle of the excursion trains.

Ellis D. Atwood met with a tragic accident and died in 1950.
Thereafter the Edaville RR entered a period of minimum maintenance
until the whole project was purchased in 1956 by F. Nelson Blount.
Mr. Blount has been anxious to preserve the spirit of the "empire."
He spent a small fortune in repairing equipment and road bed, building a new station and parking lot at the north end of the plantation
and enlarging the railroad museum, which was installed originally by
Burton Logan and who is now the curator. The new station is at Cranberry Junction and all visitors to the Edaville go thither, take the
trains to Edaville station itself where the railroad museum is located
and return to Cranberry.

The new host to countless children and their parents has added
features calculated to warm the cockles of the heart. Leaving Cranberry Junction the steam train of long ago passes Santa's Castle and
reaches Peacedale, a miniature New England village. Over towards
the big reservoir is the Cross of the Thousand Bulbs. Leaving Peacedale, one passes the Village of Churches, the swimming pool and the
picnic area. At Edaville the diversions are many: fire truck rides, open
air display of old main line live steamers, gift shop, railroad museum
and engine house. Beyond Edaville Station is Cranberry Valley and
the Reservoir station. Cranberry bogs need lots of sand and water
and here is the main supply of the latter. Beyond Reservoir, the train
whistle is blown twice in honor of Edaville's founder, Ellis D. Atwood.
Sunset Vista is the next station; and at Cranberry Cove, the final stop
before the new terminal, the train passenger can see Rudolph the
reindeer with a background of a thousand bulbs. With all these diversions it is no wonder that one night before Christmas in 1957, three
trains carried 13,104 passengers between the hours of 1:00 P.M. and
11:00 P.M. A total of 250,000 visitors enjoyed their rides and reveries
during that year.

F. Nelson Blount is collecting, by gift or purchase, live steamers
from all over the United States. The Boston and Maine RR has given
a 2-6-0 engine with four coaches. They have also donated a 4-6-2
Pacific which is currently undergoing repairs at the Concord, New
Hampshire repair shop. Mr. Blount has purchased a Standard Climax

Ex-Bridgton & Harrison R. R. No. 7 now on the Edaville Railroad, with a construction drag out on the line for general track maintenance.

Locomotives No's. 4 and 3 dragging a ten-car passenger train over the rails of the Edaville Railroad, South Carver, Massachusetts.

Locomotive No. 8 2-4-4 of the Edaville line, ex-No. 8 of the late Bridgton & Harrison of Maine, somewhat altered from its original appearance.

A study in contrast. On the left, ancient mogul (2-6-0) locomotive No. 1455 late of the Boston & Maine R. R., now a permanent exhibit on the Edaville R. R. premises. On the right is ex-Monson R. R. No. 3 built by Vulcan Iron Works in 1913, still busily steaming around the Edaville main, doing double duty hauling passengers and on occasion dropping down to the more menial tasks that are a daily part of every railroad's activities.

from a lumber road in West Virginia; a 2-8-0 from a road in New Jersey; and two former Southern Pacific locomotives which for the past thirty years have been operating at a sugar factory in Erath, Louisiana. One of these engines is a 4-4-0 Baldwin, built in 1887, and the other is a Cooke 4-6-0 built in 1893. Handsome standard-gauge equipment, they are currently in the Lafayette shops undergoing a face-lift before being shipped to South Carver.

Anaconda Copper has presented Edaville with three 30-inch-gauge saddle tank engines, two for preservation as they are and one to be sectionalized. Motor operated and on display in the museum, the old saddle tank will demonstrate what made live steamers tick in the great Age of Steam.

In addition to the Edaville's acquisitions, the Railway and Locomotive Historical Society has moved its entire museum collection to Edaville on permanent loan. What is the Baker Library's loss at Harvard University is the Edaville's gain. The collection has been at Baker for the past thirty years. Meanwhile the hunt for unusual types of locomotives goes on apace. Blount and his partner, Richardson, have recently been in Mexico, running down rumors of antique live steamers worthy of a place in the museum. One acquisition, an old steam roller, was put to good use on the roads around Edaville. Sullivan Trail Coal Company has donated a 42-inch-gauge saddle tank.

The museum is bursting at the seams with railroadiana. And there are a few sideshows too. Mr. Blount owns the largest known collection of Kentucky rifles. There are 575 of them, and more than 200 on display in the Gun Room. As high as the jezail of India's North-west Frontier, the Kentucky rifle is evocative of an age that pre-dates the "two-foot empire."

For the children it is the sideshows and features that make a visit to the Edaville RR memorable. For those a little more along in years, especially the railway enthusiasts, it is the old steam-hauled trains that provide the main attraction. In September, the cranberries are harvested and an Edaville "float boat" skims along the flooded bogs to stir up loose berries dropped by the pickers. It is propelled by an airplane engine and propeller. But such a touch of modernism cannot dispel the atmosphere of the "empire." The work train is still hauled sometimes by No. 3, which came from the little Monson RR—"Two by Six," they called it because it was two feet wide and six miles long. Smaller than the No. 7 or No. 8, she weighs only eighteen tons and musters a hundred and sixty pounds of steam. What images return when she steams along! The caboose came from the Sandy River RR

The contractors' locomotives section of the outdoor exhibition of steam locomotives at the Edaville Railroad grounds. One of the above engines is to be cut in half longitudinally to show how a steam locomotive works.

Christmas Day, double-headed passenger train on the Edaville Railroad, 1957. The largest passenger business in a single day on the line kept two trains busy accommodating the crowds as fast as they could load and unload. The locomotives here are No's. 4 and 3.

Edaville Museum

Locomotives No's. 8 and 3, engineers Blount and Richardson "up", with a mixed consist railfan special climbing Mt. Urann on Sunday, December 18th, 1955. The engines are respectively, ex-Brigton & Harrison and ex-Monson railroads of Maine.

and has a cupola. Cranberry bogs are hard task-masters but a work train with a Monson engine and a Sandy River caboose is an attractive one to man, or to whistle at in passing. George E. Mansfield, who loved his "two-footers," especially the old 2-4-4T Baldwins of the Bridgton & Saco River, would have approved the preservation of all these "empire" relics. His is a pervasive influence at Edaville because he was a trainman as well as a promoter.

The grave of Ellis D. Atwood lies against Route 58 on the eastern boundary of the Edaville plantation. It is within earshot of the engines which whistle twice in his memory. It is a ritual that is never forgotten, for in preserving a small fragment of Mansfield's "two-foot empire" Mr. Atwood has given the world a living chapter of railroad history, with emphasis on miniature lines.

No. 173 of the Carolwood-Pacific Railroad is named *Lilly Belle* in honor of Mrs. Walt Disney. She is a ⅛-scale miniature of the famed old Central Pacific locomotive of the same number and steams along a 7⅞-inch-gauge track on the Disney estate in Beverly Hills. The locomotive burns coal, operates on a head of 125 lbs. of steam and was built at the Burbank Studios of Walt Disney Productions.

The dinkey-engined Western mining train of the Rainbow Mountain Mining and Exploration Company on a tour of the arid, cactus-studded Rainbow desert of Disneyland.

CHAPTER V

MAGIC KINGDOM OF THE RAILS

The Santa Fe and Disneyland Railroad

ASK ANY CHILD the world over where the "Magic Kingdom" is, the land of storybook fantasy and frontier, and he is more than likely to reply: "Disneyland." At Anaheim, in Southern California, the Magic Kingdom is something actual which can be experienced in the here and now, and not just dreamed about or listened to. Adults catch a wild contagion from the very moment they step inside Disneyland with their children. Before their very eyes the storybook fantasy takes shape and substance.

Not least of the Magic Kingdom's properties are the miniature railways. They are many and varied: futuristic Viewliners, Western mining trains and the Casey Jr. trains made up of animal cars, chariots and calliope. But to keep within the terms of reference of this book, which is to tell the story of some of the outstanding steam-hauled miniature railways of the world, it is proposed to confine this story to the Santa Fe and Disneyland RR whose tracks encircle the whole park area itself.

By way of introduction to this railroad, which is one of the hardest worked and best maintained in the world, it should perhaps be mentioned that Mr. Disney is a railroader of long and excellent standing. He started his railroad career as a young "news butch" on the Missouri, Kansas and Texas RR and the Missouri Pacific RR, running out of Kansas City near where he was born. His experience with model railroading came with the construction of a Lionel train layout for his young nephew. The second step was the planning of an outdoor railway for himself in the present decade.

At this stage of planning Mr. Disney found among his employees a number of ardent railroad fans who had had experience with steam locomotives. Books and photographs were furnished by his fellow enthusiasts. Libraries and the shelves of bookdealers were combed throughout the country. Added to this large accumulation of data were blueprints from the Southern Pacific RR files. After the working

No. 1 would hardly recognize itself in this brand new boiler, pilot and engine truck, a fresh coat of paint and, more important still, a new number—3, coupled to the close-car consist. No. 3's new job will be to haul the picnic train of open cars.

The Santa Fe & Disneyland No. 3 when it had a "working job" down in Louisiana with Godchaux Sugar Co. as that company's No. 1. The capstack and engine truck are missing in this photo, these facilities being added in Burbank to create the atmosphere sought for the locomotive's new position of hauling human freight instead of sugar cane.

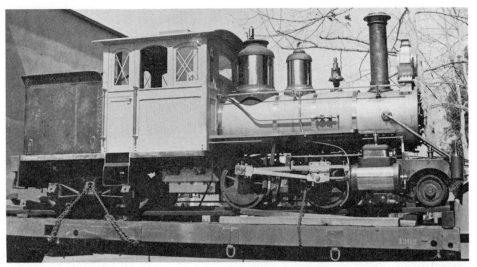

Rebuilt No. 3 on a flatbed trailer at Burbank in March, 1958, about to leave for Disneyland and placement on the narrow gauge line which circles that enchanting area.

The boiler lagging completed on the boiler of rebuilt 2-4-4 locomotive No. 3 and ready for the sheet steel jacket and banding which give the engine its high sheen. In the Victorian days of railroading, this jacket gave the fireboy a good workout as he polished it with tallow and old rags after his regular day's work. And for this effort he drew no pay.

First try-out on the rails for the newly-built cars, the eagle eye being none other than the master mechanic as the train backs up the line.

Removing the stencil from the clerestory ceiling of the passenger car. This work was multi-color in quite intricate designs in the old days.

drawings were made at the Disney Studios, the architect of the Magic Kingdom came to the shop, learned to operate machine tools, and made some of the parts himself. He was going to call his own railway the Carolwood-Pacific RR and he fashioned two box cars and cattle cars and the wooden caboose.

The first stretch of this private line was laid down in December, 1950, to a 7¼-inch-gauge at the Disney estate in Beverly Hills. Eleven switches and one crossover were required for the 1200 feet of track of the "Fairweather Route," as it was called. A further track extension was built in May 1951, making a total of 2600 feet. Motive power and rolling stock consisted of a one-eighth scale miniature of the famed old Central Pacific locomotive No. 173 in its original colors, six gondolas; and freight, cattle cars and a caboose. Both motive power and rolling stock represented the 1872-1880 period. No. 173 is named *Lilly Belle* in honor of Mrs. Disney. The "Fairweather Route" is very scenic and Mr. Disney often adopts the role of "hogger" at the head end of the train as it steams through cuts and tunnels and across bridges and trestles.

Expanding this hobby into the bigger operations of the Santa Fe and Disneyland RR is not a thing most men would attempt. But a man who can work with his hands at the exacting tasks of making machined parts for miniature railways is not to be daunted by a larger scale of things. The architect had emerged as a railroadian, fully fledged, his mind able to encompass all the problems posed by a 36-inch-gauge railroad with 9,000 feet of track.

Drawings for the *C. K. Holliday* and the *E. P. Ripley*, the first two locomotives, were based on *Lilly Belle*, and from photographs of the various engines on display at Griffith Park. The sketches, patterns and other details were completed at the Burbank Studios; and the fabrication, wheels, frames, boiler and other parts were farmed out. Then all parts were shipped down to Disneyland, and the Round House crew began their final assembly. The insulation on the boiler, the sand domes and the steam domes were made in Disneyland, the cab and the stack were made at the Studio and assembled in the machine shop.

The *C. K. Holliday*, named after the founder of the Santa Fe Railroad, hauls the freight train and is a Southern Pacific type diamond stacker. The *E. P. Ripley*, which is named after another of the Santa Fe's presidents, hauls the "varnish" or passenger train and is an aristocratic looking cap-stack locomotive. The passenger train consists of four coaches, one observation car and a combination car.

The Santa Fe and Disneyland Railroad stations are keyed to their surroundings. Frontierland depot is built in Eighteenth Century, Western style, and affords a fitting gateway to the Frontier features of Disneyland.

The *E. P. Ripley,* an aristocratic cap-stack locomotive, waits at the main Disneyland depot for the "highball" to haul a full load of passengers along the 36-inch gauge Santa Fe and Disneyland Railroad.

A contrast in design between the cap-stack *E. P. Ripley* *circa* 1890, and the Viewliner built especially for the Grand Canyon Diorama *circa* 1958!

The Casey Jr. circus "special" is for the small fry, but when the Greek goddess of music takes over and calliope is the order of the day, the old-timers go along too!

No. 2 out on the line with two cars of the passenger consist for a workout in June 1955 before Disneyland was completed. This was the locomotive's first trial run on the newly laid track.

The *C. K. Holliday* hauls the freight train and is an old Southern Pacific type diamond-stacker. The freight is just as popular with children as the "varnish," or passenger train.

The newest Disneyland train is the Excursion, built specially to carry visitors through the new Grand Canyon Diorama. Composed of five open cars, which will carry up to 325 passengers, the Excursion train is hauled by a most interesting locomotive. Named the *Fred Gurley* in honor of the chairman of the board of the Santa Fe, the engine was originally built for a New Orleans plantation owner by the Baldwin Company in 1894. Located for Disneyland by Gerald Best, vice-president of the Railway and Locomotive Historical Society, she had been hauling sugar cane on the Lafourete Raceland & Longport Railway in Louisiana; and under Roger Broggie, head of the Walt Disney Studio's machine shop, she was completely rebuilt.

In railroading terms, the *Fred Gurley* is a 2-4-4T type and the *C K. Holliday* and *E. P. Ripley* are 4-4-0's. Their mint condition each morning is a tribute to the backstage operations of the round house. Morning hours are spent steaming up the boilers; and after tie-up at night the engine crews leave their charges with the maintenance crew which begins complete inspection, cleaning, lubrication and repair. Repairs are made as necessary to the rolling stock. This complete and careful servicing has resulted in a record of not more than 30 minutes lost in operating time since the park opened. This is an enviable record and one hard to beat, even by a Class I railroad.

WED Enterprises, Inc. owns and operates all of these Santa Fe and Disneyland RR trains and has about 70 people on the payroll as engine crews and ticket sellers. Additional crews are made up of Disneyland Inc. personnel. The three trains, one passenger, one freight and one excursion, are authentic in every respect and have carried, since opening day, July 17, 1955, over 4 million passengers. The visitor has a good choice in accommodations and the excursion train open cars, designed and built at the Burbank Studio and patterned after the so-called "Narragansett Cars," are making a bold bid for the most popular mode of travel.

Below the mile and a quarter loop of track, which runs along a fill most of the way, all Disneyland is laid out before the eyes. All three of the main line trains may be boarded at any one of the four stations for the grand tour circling the Park and through the Grand Canyon. These stations are keyed to their surroundings: Frontierland has an Eighteenth Century Western-style depot; Fantasyland is appropriately designed; and Tomorrowland provides a glimpse into the ultra-modern railroad station of the future. At the ornate, 1890-era main depot—the entrance to Disneyland—the elevation is given as 138 feet and the population as 5,000,000. To serve a five million popu-

Low and sleek, the Viewliner speeds travelers over the Santa Fe right-of-way between Fantasyland and Tomorrowland. Designed for speed, it enters into the spirit of things and slows to allow the passengers a good look at the Motor Boat Cruise waterway.

This close-up of the rebuilt No. 3 reveals its fine detail and workmanship and the "spit and polish" which was characteristic of most road engines in the final decades of the last century.

lation, any railroad would have to work overtime! The Santa Fe and Disneyland RR track is probably the most traveled in the whole wide world.

From the elevation of this grand tour the traveler can see the other trains: the two sleek, futuristic Viewlanders which speed passengers over the Santa Fe right-of-way between Fantasyland and Tomorrowland; two dinky-engined Western mining trains of the Rainbow Mountain Mining and Exploration Company which carry visitors in open topped gondola cars over the arid, cactus-studded Rainbow desert and through the colorful Rainbow Caverns in Frontierland; and last but not least the Casey Jr. trains which carry children to Storybookland. The main line trains are operated according to a standard book of rules, but on the Casey Jr. the giddy calliope music takes over and the element of fantasy is too strong for the miniature railroadian. He needs to get his feet back firmly on the real, steam-hauled trains.

The personnel who help operate the Santa Fe and Disneyland RR get as much pleasure out of the live steamers as the visitors. To a man like Earl Vilmer, the mention of the words "steam trains" has been like the clang of a fire bell to a retired fire horse. Mr. Vilmer has been a steam man all his life. He helped build a vital link through Persia during World War II when the United States took over from the British the problem of working more and faster freight trains. With the trend towards diesels, he had just about decided to seek fresh pastures outside railroads when the Disneyland opportunity presented itself. The bell rang and the old firehorse jumped! Harley Ilgen is another professional railroader whose experience Mr. Disney has tapped. Mr. Ilgen was test engineer for the passenger and freight train.

There are many others whose devotion to little steam locomotives has played a vital part in bringing the Magic Kingdom to earth—and then transporting daily a multitude of people along its steam trails.

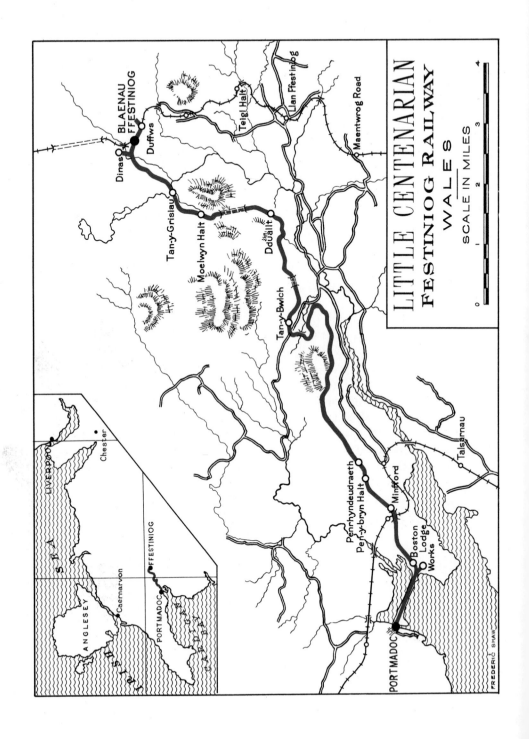

LITTLE CENTENARIAN
FESTINIOG RAILWAY
WALES
SCALE IN MILES

BLAENAU
FFESTINIOG
Dinas
Duffws
Tan-y-Grisiau
Moelwyn Halt
Dduallt
Tan-y-Bwlch
Teigl Halt
Llan Ffestiniog
Maentwrog Road
Penrhyndeudraeth
Pen-y-bryn Halt
Minfford
Boston
Lodge
Works
PORTMADOC
Talsarnau

LIVERPOOL
Chester
ANGLESEY
Caernarvon
FFESTINIOG
PORTMADOC
IRISH SEA
CARDIGAN BAY

FREDERIC SHAW

CHAPTER VI

LITTLE CENTENARIAN

The Festiniog Railway

THE FESTINIOG RAILWAY in Wales expired once in 1946, but it was an unconscionable time a-dying. The Lynton and Barnstable Railway in North Devon, England, died in 1935, but there was something in the mental and moral climate of that era that refused to heed the spectacle of a lovely little railway in its death throes.

That the Festiniog was revived before the irreversible processes of mortification had taken place is probably attributable to a new mental climate in 1950 when enough railroad enthusiasts and others interested in Britain's heritage of the narrow gauge banded together. By efforts the degree of which is hard to judge without an actual visit, they put the railway back on its feet.

The wreath that lay on the Lynton and Barnstable Railway inscribed "perchance it is not dead but sleepeth" should have adorned the Festiniog. Today, despite the ravages of nature in a climate that is excellent for growing things but tough on derelict wood and metal, the "Little Centenarian" clearly shows how fine a piece of engineering it is. A sub-standard gauge was not taken as an excuse for sub-standard track, motive power or equipment. *Taliesin*, professionally rebuilt, is not merely a locomotive of unique design but also a motive power unit of no mean order, whose vigorous exhausts suggest other parts of the world where the narrow gauge carries traffic of main line proportions.

The other spectacular piece of restoration, *Prince*, takes us back to an era when the railway map of Britain was still unfolding. After five rebuildings, parts of *Prince* must be like the traditional sailor's jacknife which had had three new handles and four new blades. The main frames, the tender and the "goodwill of the business" date back to 1863 and probably make her the oldest steam locomotive in passenger service. The design of *Prince* was quite fundamental to narrow gauge history and paved the way for the great growth of sub-standard gauge the world over.

R. W. Kidner

A gravity slate train in the old days of Festiniog Railway operation. The rear unit was a "dandy" wagon which returned the horses to Portmadoc for the next upward haul of empty cars to Blaenau Festiniog.

The Festiniog came into being in 1836 as a more efficient means of transporting slate from the upland quarries at Blaenau Festiniog. Hitherto, from quarry to quay on the River Dwyryd, the slate was carried on the backs of ponies and donkeys and in farm carts, and transhipment was effected by local men into 6-ton sailing vessels known as Philistines. These quays were at the limit of navigation and the Philistines carried the slate from the estuary to a point where facilities existed for reloading into ocean-going sailing craft. Records of such commerce go back to the beginning of the Eighteenth Century.

Toward the end of the Eighteenth Century, William Alexander Madocks built a massive sea wall to stop the encroachment of the tides across the Traeth Mawr and so reclaimed the eastern part of the Glaslyn estuary. Known locally as the "Cob", the embankment was begun in 1809 and finished in 1811. A lock gate to control the tides was built at the northern end. The swift Glaslyn tides scoured a deep channel; and Madocks, in conjunction with a young man named Samuel Holland who managed a quarry at Festiniog, commenced to build a small harbor in the new channel. The Philistines were naturally opposed to the scheme, but it offered superior facilities to their transhipment on the River Dwyryd and they commenced to sail into the new harbor of Port Madoc.

Shipbuilding facilities soon followed and Portmadoc ships became world famous. Shipowners formed their own insurance company and one company maintained regular sea-borne contact with Liverpool. When ships returned in ballast it was deposited on a rocky promontory behind Holland's Wharf. A wharf was also built on the other side of the promontory, and when the ballast was unloaded between the two, a new breakwater protecting the harbor was formed. It was on this new promontory that the Festiniog station was built, standing on materials brought from the four corners of the world in Portmadoc ships.

The first form of rail transport in the area was across the embankment or Cob which Madocks built. It was a horse-tramway used to transport stone for construction of this wall, 400 feet wide at the base and 30 feet wide at the top. Over twenty years later horses were still in the minds of the slate producers and port authorities when the railroad from Blaenau Festiniog to Portmadoc was first mooted. The opposition was strong, for the technical difficulties were formidable and the Philistines saw great inroads into their water-borne traffic of slate.

But a man arose from the controversy who had the courage and imagination to tackle something new. James Spooner, a well known

A Festiniog train proceeding from the Cob—the massive sea wall built 1809-1811 by William Alexander Madocks—to the temporary upper terminal at Tan-y-Bwlch, seven miles from Portmadoc station. Across this estuary of the Glaslyn River impressive views are obtained of Snowdonia, the Welsh mountain range whose foothills the little railway traverses.

civil engineer at the time, secured in 1832 the Royal Assent to build a railroad of 60 centimeters gauge, approximately one foot eleven and five-eighths inches between rail heads, and in February, 1833, a new era of railroad construction was ushered in.

Behind the massive Cob is the mile-wide estuary of the Glaslyn River which stretches for miles north and east to the mountain range known as Snowdonia. Through the great ramp of the foothills was to run the Festiniog Railway.

Steam power was not even considered. The line was to be a horse-drawn tramway, traversing impressive hills of volcanic origin and connecting the quarries at Blaenau Festiniog with the Cob to carry slate to the waiting ships at Portmadoc. The difference in elevation between the terminals was seven hundred feet, and many great engineering problems confronted Spooner. He had to by-pass one — the bastion of a great hill called Moelwyn which stood in the path of the railroad. Funds were insufficient to bore through Moelwyn until 1840. Initially, dobbin hauled the empty cars up to the quarries; and they returned, fully laden, by force of gravity, dobbin riding at the rear of the slate train in what was known as a "dandy" wagon. Cars were equipped with hand-operated brakes, manned by brakemen to control speed. Dobbin must have enjoyed watching them work. Braking cars loaded with slate, which weighs like lead, is no mean task.

Despite the light rail used and the primitive tractive and braking efforts, the little road was built on the soundest engineering principles. In 1846 the original track was lifted and replaced by 30-pound rail and wooden ties, laid to a standard that could hardly be bettered by Class I railroads.

The steam locomotive had come into use in England about the time the Festiniog was first laid down. And when James Spooner died in 1859, he was succeeded as engineer by his son, Charles Easton Spooner, who had long felt dobbin an anachronism. He was fond of horses but he couldn't let his affection stand in the way of progress. The increasing slate business warranted the conversion to steam traction with the least possible delay. Although the foremost railroad engineers of the day, among them Stephenson and Brunel, were convinced a two-foot gauge was impracticable for live steamers, the younger Spooner persuaded his sponsors otherwise. Like his father, his thought was in advance of his time and by 1863 two small 0-4-0 engines emerged from the works of George England of New Cross, London named the *Prince* and the *Princess*. Each weighed only 7½ tons. They were so successful that in the following year the *Mountaineer* and *Palmerston* were placed in service.

Any one of the locomotives could easily haul fifty empty cars up the circuitous grade to the quarries and demonstrated for all time the efficacy of steam power for slim gauge work. The demand for scheduled passenger services soon followed, such services having hitherto been restricted to the standard gauges. It was a radical departure from the concept of railroad safety when the Festiniog in January 1865 started regular passenger service. Not least of the "Little Centenarian's" achievements in this respect was the introduction of the first double-truck ("bogie") passenger cars in Britain. Traffic increased so rapidly that further motive power was ordered: two heavier and more powerful locomotives ensued, *Welsh Pony* and *Little Giant*.

Exchange sidings with standard gauge rail lines were finally built at Minffordd where much of the slate was transferred. In 1867, four additional miles of main line were added to the Festiniog, extending its upper end to the village of Llan Ffestiniog. This extension was separately owned by an independent, although operated by what has come to be known as the world's oldest public narrow-gauge railway.

In the late 1860's an event came to pass which was to have a great impact upon the fortunes of the "Little Centenarian", as well as the railroad world in general. A noted engineer had designed a double-ended locomotive, unique in that it had two articulated engine chassis under a single boiler. The cab and fire-box were "amidships", so to speak. Robert Fairlie, the engineer in question was, like the Spooners, ahead of his time. His critics were outspoken. In their opinion it was folly enough to build such a locomotive in standard gauge; to build a live steamer for so small a track gauge as two-feet was nothing more than a jest. In view of this the first of these engines *Little Wonder*, of 0-4-4-0 type, built by George England, staggered the pundits of the period by hauling a heavy train up the steepest grade. To rub it in, the *Little Wonder* was stopped on a grade, its steam pressure greatly reduced, and a fresh start made with the same heavy load. The test reverberated around the railroad world. India, New Zealand and South Africa built railroads as a direct result in the same narrow gauge.

One of the visitors to the Festiniog was George E. Mansfield who took back with him to his native New England not only mental pictures of the scenic delights of woodland, river, volcanic hills and waterfalls but plans for the road and rolling stock of the Billerica and Bedford Railroad in Massachusetts, thereby bowing in the era of the 2-foot empire of New England.

The first Fairlie was given the name *Little Wonder*. In 1872 a second Fairlie was ordered with the name *James Spooner*. At that time the track was relaid with 48½ pound rail. The third addition to the Fairlie stud was the *Merddin Emrys* in 1885. *Livingston Thompson* was the last double Fairlie which, with the original *Taliesin* (single ended), made a total of five.

The advent of World War I proved a major setback to successful operation. Between the wars, the price of slate and unwise mergers coupled to bring disaster. The Festiniog closed for passenger service in 1939. A few slate trains continued to work between the Blaenau quarries and the standard gauge at Minffordd, but the signaling and telegraph systems were allowed to rust away, along with track and rolling stock. When the decision came, in 1946, to abandon all operations, locomotives and rolling stock were left literally standing where each unit happened to be at the moment. Welshmen, who sing like angels whenever two or three are gathered together, lamented in silence. Their feelings were too deep for song.

But the newspapers were more vocal as time went on. An editorial in the Liverpool *Daily Post* of October 1948 said:

> It is now two years since the stout-hearted little Fairlie engine made its asthmatic assault upon the steep gradient that leads from Portmadoc through poetry to Festiniog town.
>
> By now the rust and weeds have pronounced their *Nunc Dimittis* over the toy railway—a toy with a serious purpose which doesn't seem likely ever to function again.
>
> No more shall palpitating tourists be locked in those fearsome little trucks and be whisked thirteen miles upwards through Dante-esque tunnels, where the wind shrieked and the sulphur fumes clutched their throats, and quick glimpses of beauty moved their hearts.
>
> Wasn't it an English poet who said that a lifetime in Maentwrog's valley would pass with the fleetness of a summer's day?
>
> Down at Portmadoc a pitiful air of decay grips the headquarters of the railway. The green badge of ruin is fixed on the rolling stock. Even that quaint railway hearse that was once in commission to bring the dead for burial from the hill-flung farms, is itself now at the end of its tether.
>
> At one time this railway yielded handsome profits. It was popular. Even when the tourists didn't come, the quarrymen from Portmadoc went to work at Festiniog in the trucks with iron bars across the windows.

Richard Pennoyer

The Fairlie Patent *James Spooner* No. 8 built by Avonside Engine Co. in its final form. As originally built it had front and rear weatherboards only, the cab pictured herewith being added by the Festiniog shops at Boston Lodge. Also as originally built the *James Spooner* was equipped with boiler-mounted sand domes, each with a bell mounted on its top. The four cylinders of this engine were each 8½"x14", drivers 2 ft. 8 inches diameter, boiler pressure 140 lbs., rigid wheel base of each bogie was 4 ft. 6 inches and total wheel base 18 ft. 8 inches. Tractive effort was 5,410 lbs. The driving bogies were pivotted off-center to counteract the weight of the cylinders. Most interesting was the fact that locomotive *Taliesin* No. 9 was an exact duplicate of one-half of the Fairlie engine *Spooner* except for a half-enclosed cab and bunker, supported by a 4-wheel truck.

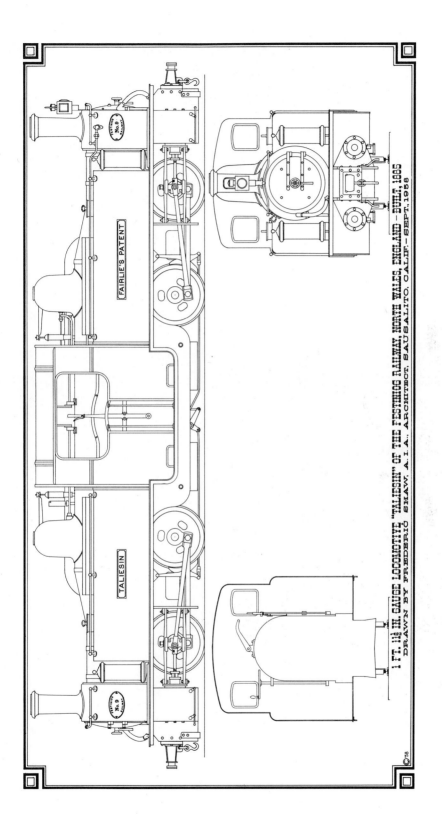

FAIRLIE'S PATENT

TALIESIN

1 FT. 11½ IN. GAUGE LOCOMOTIVE "TALIESIN" OF THE FESTINIOG RAILWAY, NORTH WALES, ENGLAND — BUILT, 1885
DRAWN BY FREDERIC SHAW, A.I.A., ARCHITECT, SAUSALITO, CALIF. — SEPT. 1958

The incomparable Fairlie locomotive *Taliesin*. Here she is undergoing trials after a complete overhaul.

In one truck a Bible class would be held, with some bearded patriarch in charge. In the next one, possibly, a card "school" with the glint of coin as the stakes changed hands.

Now it would take some thousands of pounds to renew the permanent way, worn beyond safe use, and to gild with freshness the rolling stock. The proposition seems hardly an economic one.

For six years the Festiniog Railway lay abandoned until, undoubtedly nettled by the rejuvenation of the Talyllyn, a group of railway enthusiasts obtained control of the little line, a new board of directors was appointed and plans laid for the revival of the forerunner of all narrow gauge operation throughout the world. There were two organizations concerned with the line — the Festiniog Railway Company which operated the system as the statutory body; and the Festiniog Railway Society Limited, a company limited by guarantee which existed in that form to formalize financial negotiations with the operating company and to assist in providing both funds and labor.

But it wasn't until January 5, 1955 that the following news item appeared in the London *Times:*

NARROW GAUGE RAILWAY LIKELY TO RE-OPEN
VOLUNTEERS REPAIRING LINE

The Festiniog narrow-gauge railway, which was closed eight years ago, may reopen this summer. The line, which became a pattern for many miles of narrow gauge lines in the United States, is owned by the Festiniog Railway Company, the board of which consists chiefly of enthusiasts and professional railway-men, supported by the Festiniog Railway Society, which was formed in 1951. A new company known as the Festiniog (Merioneth) Railway Society Ltd. has recently been registered to acquire and hold the issued shares of the Festiniog Railway Company.

The society is calling for volunteers to help with repairs to the line, which runs for about 13 miles from Portmadoc to Blaenau Festiniog, and are sending organized parties once a month to carry out the work. . . .

Six months later the reopening of the Festiniog was an accomplished fact. Under the dateline July 29, 1955, the London *Times* reported a truly historic moment when Miss Janet Jones, the Welsh National hostess, formally reopened the line at Portmadoc. Thereafter it jogged along at ten miles an hour across the massive sea wall to Boston Lodge. It had been hoped to get the steam locomotive *Prince* to haul the train of two cream-and-green coaches. But although volunteers worked all night the sturdy veteran was not quite ready and a gasoline tractor of World War I vintage deputized instead.

R. W. Kidner

Tan-y-Bwlch station, the present (1958) upper terminal of the Festiniog Railway. The photograph was taken in 1936 and shows a train hauled by *Merddin Emrys,* one of Spooner's Fairlie locomotives which is due to return to service after a complete overhaul.

English Electric Company

Fairlie locomotive *Taliesen* as she was in 1890 when named *Livingston Thompson.* Now professionally rebuilt, the *Taliesen* is hauling happy crowds of vacationers over the Festiniog's rehabilitated mountain railway in Wales.

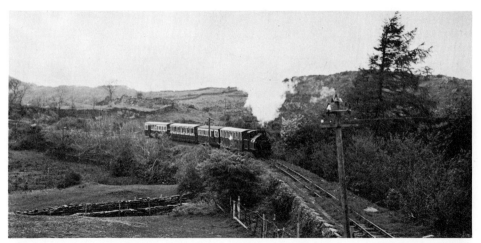

The Festiniog Railway line above Pen-y-Bryn. Not least of the slim-gauge pike's claims to fame is the fact that it was the first railway in the world to introduce double-truck passenger coaches. Charles Easton Spooner, who succeeded his father, the original engineer of the line, was responsible for this great innovation.

Members of the Festiniog Railway Society, which was formed in 1951, have succeeded so far in getting back into operation seven of the thirteen miles of the original pike, and are seen working at the Boston Lodge yards. They are determined men and need all the help they can get to reopen the rest of the line to Blaenau Festiniog, even though this will entail an alternative route three miles long to bypass the Central Electricity Authority's new reservoir above Tan-y-Bwlch.

Inside the Festiniog Railway's Boston Lodge shops *circa* 1938. In the foreground
is the frame of *Prince*. She has undergone five rebuildings since 1863 and as
presently operating is probably the oldest steam locomotive in the world today.
Behind the frame of *Prince* is *Taliesin*.

Dubbed the "Little Centenarian" by overseas visitors, the Festiniog Railway in
Wales is one of the finest pieces of railroad engineering in the world and the
precursor of the narrow-gauge lines. Here is a train steaming down towards the
Portmadoc estuary. The overhang of the rear car looks formidable. Nevertheless,
the ride is smooth and the Festiniog enjoys an almost unblemished safety record.

Two years later a special correspondent of the London *Times* reported the following, under the dateline of July 4, 1957:

FESTINIOG RAILWAY STEAMS AHEAD
PLAN TO BYPASS NEW RESERVOIR

Three years' labor of love by a group of enthusiastic amateur railwaymen (with a leavening of professionals on holiday) has put a three and a half mile stretch of the Festiniog Railway, the first narrow-gauge passenger line in Britain, back in service after lying derelict for 10 years.

By next year they will have done even better. The tourists, who have already taken the railway to their hearts—39,000 passengers were carried last year and traffic this year is twice as heavy—will then be carried up the line as far as Tan-y-Bwlch, seven miles above Portmadoc terminus. At this stage the Festiniog Railway Society's plans for further expansion have run into difficulties, for between Tan-y-Bwlch and the inland terminus of Blaenau Festiniog, two miles of the 125-year-old line will soon be submerged 16 ft. under the waters of a new reservoir being constructed for the Central Electricity Authority's first pump storage scheme to generate off-peak electricity.

Flooding Opposed

The inundation of the line was strongly opposed by the Festiniog Railway when the C.E.A. were seeking powers for the development. That, however, was in 1955 when no trains had run since the railway's closure in 1946. The society's plans to restore the line did not offer the House of Lords strong enough grounds to amend the scheme.

The Festiniog Society is now beginning negotiations for compensation from the C.E.A. With this money they plan to build an alternative line three miles long involving heavier gradients and a 600-yard tunnel. The new route has been surveyed by professional surveyors among the society's membership who consider the work can be done for about 65,000 pounds. There is hope of some help being received from Sapper units of the Territorial Army who are often glad of unusual practical training exercises.

Access to Main Line

The Society is determined that the line shall be reopened up to Blaenau, to provide access to the main line and enable British Railways to arrange circular tours. Such an achievement would re-establish the Festiniog firmly on the railway map and, members believe, kill once and for all the idea that their venture is merely a slightly inferior Talyllyn. . . .

FESTINIOG RAILWAY COMPANY

1958

TIME TABLE

WEEKDAYS ONLY, 24th MAY-27th SEPTEMBER, also 5th and 7th APRIL
SUNDAYS, 6th APRIL, 25th MAY and 3rd AUGUST
WEDNESDAYS ONLY, 9th APRIL-21st MAY and 1st-22nd OCTOBER
(See Note A)

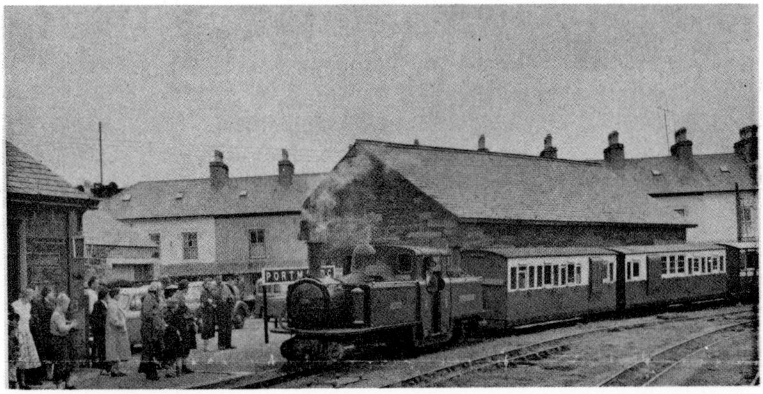

(Photo by courtesy of the English Electric Co. Ltd.)

	PWLLHELI	dep.	9S25	9E55	12.45			
	PORTMADOC (W)	arr.	9S56	10E23	1.14			
	BARMOUTH	dep.		9.25	12.20	2S40	3E45	
	MINFFORDD	arr.		10.15	1.12	3S21dd	4E36	
	PORTMADOC (W)	arr.			1.16	3S26		
				B				C
0	PORTMADOC (Harbour)	dep.		10.40	2.30		4.30	7.30
¾	PEN COB (Halt)	,,		dd	dd		dd	......
1	BOSTON LODGE (Halt)	,,		dd	dd		dd	dd
2¼	MINFFORDD (for B.R. (W))	,,		10.52	2.42		4.42	dd
3	PEN-Y-BRYN (Halt)	,,		dd	dd		dd	......
3¼	PENRHYN	,,		10.58	2.48		4.48	dd
7½	TAN-Y-BWLCH	arr.		11.25	3.15		5.15	8.10
9	DDUALLT	} Service temporarily suspended						
12	TAN-Y-GRISIAU							
13¼	BLAENAU FFESTINIOG							
0	BLAENAU FFESTINIOG	} Service temporarily suspended						
1¼	TAN-Y-GRISIAU							
4¼	DDUALLT			B				C
5¾	TAN-Y-BWLCH	dep.		11.45	3.30		5.30	8.40
10	PENRHYN	,,		12.12	3.57		5.57	dd
10¼	PEN-Y-BRYN (Halt)	,,		dd	dd		dd	......
11	MINFFORDD (for B.R.(W))	,,		12.18	4.03		6.03	dd
12¼	BOSTON LODGE (Halt)	,,		dd	dd		dd	dd
12½	PEN COB (Halt)	,,		dd	dd		dd	......
13¼	PORTMADOC (Harbour)	arr.		12.30	4.15		6.15	9.20
	PORTMADOC (W)	dep.		1.17	4.35			
	MINFFORDD	dep.		1.22	4.40		6.08	
	BARMOUTH	arr.		2.12	5.27		6.57	
	MINFFORDD	dep.			4E31		6.17	
	PORTMADOC (W)	dep.		1.20	4E40	4S32	6.20	
	PWLLHELI	arr.		1.55	5E20	5S05	7.00	

Western Region times shown apply 9th June-13th September, week-days only.

A. On Wednesdays only, 9th April-21st May and 1st-22nd October, the 3.30 train will leave Tan-y-Bwlch at 3.45 and run 15 minutes later throughout. The 4.30 from Portmadoc and 5.30 from Tan-y-Bwlch will not run.

B. Runs 30th June-13th September, week-days only, also Easter Monday, 7th April.

C. Runs Tuesday, Wednesday, Thursday and Saturday only, 8th July-6th September, also Whit Saturday and Monday, May 24th and 26th. Trains marked B and C may also run on other days by prior arrangement.

E. Except Saturdays.

S. Saturdays only.

dd Calls when required to set down on notice to the Guard at previous stopping station; passengers wishing to join should give the necessary hand signal to the Driver.

T STEPHENSON & SONS LTD., PRINTERS, PRESCOT, LANCS.

Two men supporters carried their enthusiasm to the point of embroidering antimacassars for the first-class compartments of the passenger coaches. They were Lennox Jamieson and David Ronald, Edinburgh University students.

The circular tours mentioned are important to the Festiniog. They were arranged in conjunction with the old London, Midland and Scottish Railway and the Great Western Railway. Trips from Llandudno would take the vacationer south to Blaenau Festiniog by the standard gauge Conway Valley line, by connecting Festiniog train to Portmadoc with time out for lunch, then by the now defunct Welsh Highland line to Dinas where a train would be waiting to carry passengers back to Llandudno via Bangor. There were alternative tours and it has been estimated that up to World War II between 65,000 and 75,000 passengers were carried by the Little Centenarian each year.

The line runs through countryside which is full of infinite variety: seascape and stream, green mountains, slate roofed cottages, ancient castles and piny woods, waterfalls and lake — all as the traveler leans from the window and hears that unique blast of the Fairlie's twin stacks.

It may be of interest to give a breakdown on the motive power presently in service or being reconditioned. The 0-4-0 saddle tank *Prince* is in service, together with the rebuilt 0-4-4-0 Fairlie *Taliesin*. The sister engine to the saddle tank, *Princess*, will be back in service shortly. *Welsh Pony*, another saddle tank, is expected back in service. In addition, the third of the incomparable Fairlies, *Merddin Emrys*, will soon hit the high iron of the Festiniog as it mounts towards the terminal at Blaenau Festiniog.

Note: Memberships are open to all well-wishers in any of several classifications. That's how funds are made available for the actual work of reconstruction. An enquiry addressed to the Honorary Financial Secretary, 35 Holmwood Road, Cheam, Surrey, England, will bring the necessary data. Members are recipients of frequent bulletins issued by the Society, keeping them abreast of progress.

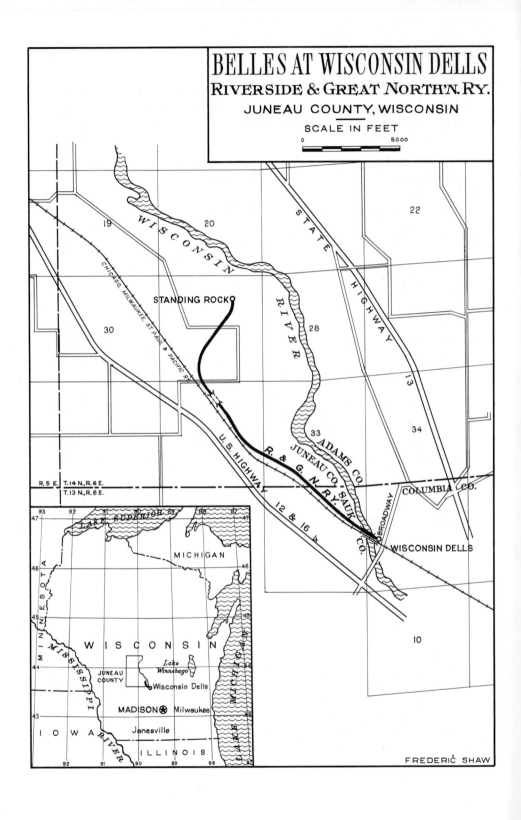

CHAPTER VII

BELLES AT WISCONSIN DELLS

The Riverside and Great Northern Railway

THE FIRST COMMON carrier in the United States resorting to the track gauge of fifteen inches is presently in being at the small and picturesque village of Wisconsin Dells on the Wisconsin River in the state of the same name. This little road, named the Riverside and Great Northern Railway, is presently two and one-half miles in extent and operates over the original grade of the old La Crosse and Milwaukee Railroad dating back to pre-Civil War days. The route was used in the opening of the great Northwest Territory, over which rode many illustrious pioneers. The preparation of this portion of the original railroad was completed about the year 1854 with mule and ox teams at a cost of approximately $100,000. With such a storied site for starting a railroad, a father and son team are making miniature railroad history.

The son, Norman K. Sandley, is a locomotive engineer on the Chicago, Milwaukee, St. Paul and Pacific Railroad and is the promoter of the Sandley Light Railway Equipment Works which operates in conjunction with the little Riverside line. However, like father, like son, is no empty aphorism, for Sandley Senior is retired from the same main line, and lends both brain and sinew to the ambitious scheme of building and operating miniature trains.

It has often been truly remarked that the really successful builder of the small steam locomotive must be equipped with more than a machine shop and skills in the use of machinery. He must be a kind of Peter Pan, possessing the secret of eternal youth and an acute eye for good design. Norman Sandley has the quality required to turn out eye-catching small locomotives. Were proof wanting, one has but to glimpse any one of the several fifteen-inch gauge steam locomotives created in his shops, now in Wisconsin Dells, but recently removed from Janesville in the same state, one hundred miles to the south.

Mr. Sandley had the good fortune to discover the stretch of surplus right-of-way belonging to the line for which he worked. It had come into being as a result of a track re-alignment. Seeing its possibilities as a right-of-way for a small gauge rail line, Sandley negotiated with the

What section gang boasts of its own steam engine to travel to and from the job each day? This intriguing little 4-wheeled No. 1 of the Riverside & Great Northern Ry. with its steam driven vertical engine, adds joy to a day's work as the crew gets an easy lift home.

Machinists in the shops of the Sandley Light Railway & Equipment Works study a problem over the partly assembled chassis of 15-inch gauge locomotive No. 98. With so formidable a library as lines the wall of the shop, one would think there would be little excuse for not turning out these handsome and perfect little locomotives.

parent railroad and the land title was transferred from the big railroad to the little one. On this serpentine stretch, Sandley built two-and-one-half miles of 15-inch gauge track, using 12-lb. rail (shortly to be relaid with 16-lb. rail), all of it ballasted in the manner of Class I railroads. Stations and a few of the other buildings have been erected adequate for present requirements. Extension of the main line too is in the back of Sandley's mind. This would take the rails in extensions from each end to Broadway, Wisconsin Dells, at the southern end and to Standing Rock, a natural amphitheatre and site of a proposed Indian village, at the northern end. About one and one-half miles of extra trackage are involved.

Another Sandley project is a small old-time town devised in the manner of the mid-Victorian era, complete with the cracker barrel grocery, a blacksmith shop, curiosity shop and such other establishments one might expect to find in an antique village.

Now that the line is in full swing, carrying passengers along the scenic route, trains are despatched in the accepted manner of the old-time railroads. Trains leave according to the schedules of a printed timetable. It is no amusement park procedure of waiting for the passenger cars to fill up. When train time comes, it's a cry of "BOARD!" even though cars might be half empty and latecomers within hailing distance. Time and tide and the Riverside wait for no man!

Norman Sandley has a tremendous admiration for the famed Romney, Hythe and Dymchurch Light Railway in England which daily throughout the year traverses the shingle and marsh of the Kentish coast. The Romney is also a fifteen-inch gauge steam operated passenger and freight line founded in 1926 by Capt. J. E. P. Howey. Sandley has borrowed from usual English locomotive builders' practice, the use of plate frames rather than the bar type common to American built locomotives. Other details of British motive power which Sandley admires and has adopted are the 20-spoke driving wheels (in the U. S. it is 16), the short, curvaceous smokestack and the cylinder block. On the other hand, the square headlight is somewhat of a concession to ancient U. S. practice. This type of beacon was almost universally common to locomotives of the Pennsylvania Railroad. Such odd features as those just recited have the virtue at least of being unusual and eye-catching. One other oldtime practice is the color scheme of Sandley locomotives, a habit dropped by American railroads nearly three-quarters of a century ago. As these colorful little locomotives steam along the main line, none can fail to thrill at their speed and power.

The first diesel manufactured for the Milwaukee Zoo by the Sandley Light Railway Equipment Works, Inc., of Wisconsin Dells, Wis. The locomotive is 15-inch gauge, powered with a 40 H.P. Waukesha diesel engine, is equipped with one hydraulic motor on each axle, has a Vickers control valve, air brakes and is 15'-11" in length, 2'-8" wide and 5'-0" high. This unit of motive power is the second manufactured by the company for the Zoo Line.

A 15-inch gauge work car that any boy would like to push around. Note the water barrel with its long-handled cup. Shovel and hammer set the scale.

Handsome Atlantic type locomotive No. 128 *North Star* of the 15″ gauge Riverside & Great Northern Railway of Wisconsin Dells, Wis. The valve gear is Sandley rotary. Cylinders are 4½″x6″; valves 2½″ diameter, with 1½″ travel; drivers 20½″ diameter, engine truck wheels 10″; trailer wheels 12″; weight, engine and tender, 9,500 lbs., height 4′-2″; width 2′-8″; overall length 21′-0″; tractive force 783 lbs., tender capacity, water 200 gals., coal 300 lbs.

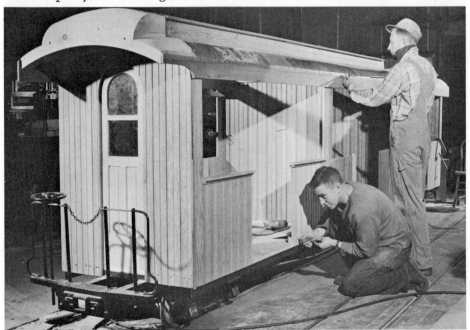

Versatility would appear to be aptly applied to the personnel of the Sandley Light Railway & Equipment Works at Wisconsin Dells, Wis., as these two men fashion an old style wooden day coach. It will seat 12 passengers.

Norman K. Sandley rightly has a pleased look on his countenance as he awaits the "Highball" from the train conductor. The train is about to pull out from East Station for a northbound journey over the rails of the Riverside & Great Northern Railway. The steam dome still lacks its finished top.

The interesting backhead of 15-inch-gauge locomotive No. 98, showing the simple controls needed. The glove on the right indicates the scale.

The accompanying photographs of the locomotive shops will give some idea of the building activity. New locomotives projected and under way include three additional 4-4-0's, one a diamond stacker, another a cap-stacker and the third a balloon-stacker. The balloon-stacker, No. 82, is for the Milwaukee Zoo and the cap-stacker is for the New Orleans Audubon Zoo. Another balloon-stacker, the No. 54, will join the stable of the Riverside and Great Northern Railway. Also building is an Atlantic for the Milwaukee Zoo with the number 126. In what little spare time father and son have, a new 32-foot turntable is being fashioned to supplant the existing one.

Complete engine terminal facilities are planned, to include stall brick roundhouse, running repair shop, coal shed, cinder pit, sand house, in and outgoing tracks, drop pit, thru stall and Foreman's office. The motivating force behind all this work may be summed up in Norman Sandley's own words: "When the diesel was merely a threat and not a fact, we started to sense the value of preserving the art of steam locomotive manufacturing and operation."

The official opening day for the Riverside and Great Northern was May 15, 1958. Events have since proved that the little railway can pay its own way in every respect, thereby giving the Sandleys a legitimate business right to pursue their great and abiding interest. The twelve new passenger cars of open platform type which are now building will be pressed into service at the earliest opportunity. Similar cars have already been built for the Milwaukee Zoo.

The round trip, costing 35 cents, takes twenty minutes and penetrates such scenic grandeur that a brief note on the area may be of interest. Leaving Wisconsin Dells station, one mile from town, the train proceeds westerly through deep woods to Summit, the highest point. After leaving Summit, the train passes through a 500-foot rock cut, thence into the open and over a big fill. This type of scenery predominates almost to the outskirts of the depot called Rockdale where there are passing track facilities. At one time, the railway construction camp was located here, together with the company sawmill. As the train pulls into Rockdale station itself, it rumbles into the intense shadow of a solid rock cut 40 feet high and the refreshing coolness of damp moss.

We stop but a short time at Rockdale and proceed along the one-quarter mile curve where our stout engine can be seen on the upgrade to Deer Pass. We are now traveling due north. To the left of the open car train is one of the longest fills on the Milwaukee railroad system. On our right we can see the old Wisconsin River channel. The engine

Steel gang laying track on the right-of-way of the Riverside & Great Northern west of Rockdale, a station on the line.

Ancient and modern meet one another on the rails of the Riverside & Great Northern Ry. as the designer and builder of both locomotives stands beside his latest creation, No. 98. The Atlantic on the right is No. 128.

This handsome 15-inch-gauge Hudson, No. 1 on the builder's roster of the Riverside & Great Northern Ry. of Wisconsin is the only one of the several that line has built with bar frames. It was sold to operate in another park some time after the railroad was built and re-numbered 4001.

A local train stopped west of Summit, Wis., to take on water. This engine can attain a speed of twenty-five miles an hour hauling a loaded train of six cars.

whistles — and how that little whistle fills us with longing for the long ago of steam engines! — for Deer Pass station, named for the deer crossing both the tracks of the Milwaukee Road and our own Riverside and Great Northern. Deer Pass is a flagstop only, although this time we stop just to catch sight of a lonesome buck at the water hole off the Wisconsin River. Now on through a shallow birch and pine covered rock cut towards Bilty Falls, named in memory of Charles H. Bilty, one of the most famous locomotive designers and railroad men of this century.

With reduced speed, we pass through the station and over a stone-arched canyon. We can glimpse on the left the 70-foot cascade of sun-sparkled water to the rocks of the ever-changing Wisconsin river course. Our engine picks up speed and steams through the canyons of shadow to the depot of Deadwood. These are not the Black Hills of Wild Bill Hickock but a valley where giant ferns thrive on the mulch of dead wood.

At Deadwood the single track divides into double track as far as Western Springs, where the roundhouse, back shops, company offices and all the facilities for marking this road a peer among its fellows will eventually be located.

The Riverside and Great Northern Railroad is, in a sense, a living memorial to steam. To quote Norman Sandley again: "We think that all phases of our railroad, including the clerical, signal, B & B, maintenance of way, stores, operating and motive power departments should be completely represented, very distinctly, thus paying tribute to all the men and their theories, as well as their practices, prior to the streamlining of our once efficient railways."

Those are the words of a rugged individualist. And who is to say he is wrong?

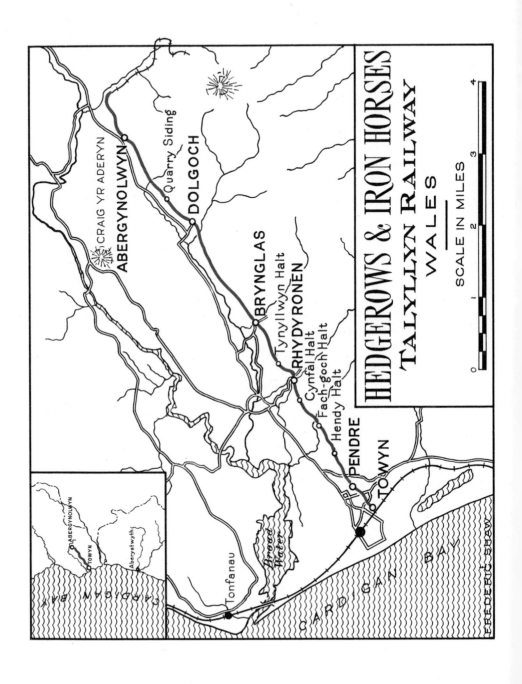

HEDGEROWS & IRON HORSES
TALYLLYN RAILWAY
WALES

SCALE IN MILES

0   1   2   3   4

CRAIG YR ADERYN

ABERGYNOLWYN

Quarry Siding

DOLGOCH

BRYNGLAS

Tynllwyn Halt

RHYDYRONEN

Cynfal Halt

Fach-goch Halt

Hendy Halt

PENDRE

TOWYN

Tonfanau

Broad Water

CARDIGAN BAY

ABERGYNOLWYN

TOWYN

Aberystwyth

CARDIGAN BAY

FREDERIC SHAW

CHAPTER VIII

HEDGEROWS AND IRON HORSES

The Talyllyn Railway

THE TALYLLYN RAILWAY, which runs for nearly seven miles up a mountain valley in Wales, enjoyed for a brief period the title of the oldest surviving steam-hauled, passenger carrying narrow gauge railway in the world. Its sister line, the Festiniog, ceased operation temporarily in 1946 and was not reopened for passenger service until July, 1955. Since the Festiniog was originally opened to passengers in 1865, a year earlier than the Talyllyn, it is conscious of its seniority; but to the Talyllyn goes the accolade for unbroken service to the present day.

Both lines have been preserved by an awakened public opinion in Britain; and it is not easy to equate the work of the enthusiasts of both lines who have done the actual job of rehabilitation. The Festiniog members had to dig deeply through the overlay of neglect to reach the solid engineering of the Spooner era; the Talyllyn members, or partisans (for naturally one must have personal preferences) faced the results of minimum maintenance on a more lightly constructed line.

Like other Welsh narrow gauge railways, it was the slate carrying industry which brought the Talyllyn Railway into being, although in this case a passenger service was envisioned at the beginning. When in 1847 John Pughe began quarrying for slate at Bryn Eglwys, an almost inaccessible cleft in the mountains above the village of Abergynolwyn, his slates had to be transported by pack ponies to the port of Aberdovey for shipment. The McConnel family, who succeeded John Pughe, quickly realized that the future of the quarry depended on more efficient transport to the coast. They met this challenge by hiring James Swinton Spooner to survey a route for a railway from the quarry down the valley of the Afon Fathew to the coast at Towyn. Spooner was, of course, the son of the engineer of the Festiniog and the brother of C. E. Spooner who introduced steam to the "Little Centenarian." The adoption of a gauge of 2 ft. 3 in. instead of the more normal 60 centimeters may possibly be explained by the gauge already in existence at the Bryn Eglwys slate quarries.

Until the final closure of the Bryn Eglwys in 1947, the fortunes of the railway and the quarry were closely linked and the same adminis-

No. 1 *Talyllyn* is seen arriving at the shops of Gibbons Bros., Ltd., Brierly Hill, Staffordshire, for a complete overhaul. She returned in June 1958 in "mint" condition, an "Old Lady" with 93 years of service who is held in the deepest regard by members.

No. 3 *Sir Haydn* in the Talyllyn shops at Pendre. To American railroaders the cosy forge must be somewhat reminiscent of Longfellow's village blacksmith shop, but all save major overhauls are undertaken in this bucolic atmosphere.

tration was responsible for both. In 1911 this joint control passed from the McConnel family to Sir Henry Haydn Jones, a notable Towyn personality who was a Member of Parliament for Merioneth for many years. Although the closure of the quarry deprived the little road of its staple traffic, causing it to operate in the red, Sir Haydn continued to maintain a passenger service throughout the summer months until his death in his eighty-seventh year. It was in this way that the Talyllynn Railway's unique record of unbroken service was set up. It was achieved at a price, however, for no money was available for essential repairs and the line was literally worked to death.

The partisans then stepped in and formed in 1950 the Talyllyn Railway Preservation Society starting on the long road back. Thanks to the generous cooperation of Sir Haydn's Executors, the new Society became responsible for operating the railway, acquiring control of the old company by means of a limited shareholding company. A year after the inception of practical work the line carried 22,000 passengers; in the following year, 1953, the total reached 30,000. And in the year ended September 28, 1957, the number of passengers carried was over 57,000. In fact, there was a net operating profit. Class I railroads of the world, please take note!

For those who knew the Talyllyn in its pre-Society days, the transformation is almost unbelievable. The visitor today can see small steam locomotives at their very best, well tended, beautifully groomed, and obviously dear to the hearts of all. Three factors have contributed to the present situation. First, the financial help received from members all over the world; secondly, the unflagging practical support of members who have contributed physical labor or valuable materials and equipment; and thirdly, the over 2,000 Society members have taken their responsibility to the public seriously. There is no "playing at trains", even though it is sometimes necessary to remind muscular young members that "too much time is spent riding in the trains when, for example, the track gangs are short handed." The atmosphere on the line is what Dr. Johnson would call "clubbable", with a warm friendliness on the part of the officials, but train operation is conducted according to the highest standards of Class I railways.

The route itself is so enchanting that it deserves a brief description. On pulling out of Wharf station, the Towyn terminal, the train passes Towyn Pendre, the original passenger depot and the location of the Company's locomotive shops, and begins its long and almost unbroken climb towards Abergynolwyn. This first section is across the

No. 2 *Dolgoch*, the middle engine in the picture, being shunted onto a waiting truck for conveyance to a Midland factory. Built in 1866 for the opening of the Talyllyn Railway, she is expected to be back in service in 1959. No. 6 *Douglas* is the engine standing on the left.

fields of open country. Until recently the engines puffed in what seemed to be a continuous green tunnel. This tunnel was in fact the overgrown hedgerows planted to keep out sheep. Nowadays the hedges have been "cut and laid", which gives them a trim appearance and provides the passengers with a constantly changing view of sea and mountain.

After passing Cynfal Halt at the summit of a long 1.5% grade the train enters Rhydyronen station, 2½ miles from the Wharf. There is a Chalybeate Spring in the wood not far from the station which an early guide book described as "of great efficacy in cases of nervous exhaustion, dyspepsia and general debility", although this attempt to popularize the place as a spa met scant success. The steepest grade on the line lifts the little train out of Rhydyronen to a summit over the Braich-y-Rhiw stream. The line then falls for a short distance then levels off for a distance. In the old days when vacationers could hire a slate wagon for the day and make the journey to Towyn by gravity, it was at this level point that gravity failed them. Such practices are not in keeping with present operations.

After a comparatively short run the train passes a grade crossing and enters Brynglas, which means "Green Hill". From the deep cutting beyond Brynglas the train puffs over a fill which gives a fine view of Cader Idris, on which mountain, it is said, a man lost overnight in the fog awakens either a bard or a madman. The valley of the Afon Fathew narrows here and the track takes up a position on a ledge cut in the steep slopes of the hills. Scenically, the approach to Dolgoch is perhaps the highlight of the journey. The first section is through woodland over a dappled track of sunlight and shadow. After a rock cut the train emerges with dramatic suddenness onto the Dolgoch viaduct, the biggest engineering work on the line. Built of brick with stone facings, the three spans carry the track over the precipitous Dolgoch ravine. One of the necessary projects of the Talyllyn Railway Preservation Society was the rebuilding of the spandril walls.

Beyond this viaduct another cut, set on a sharp curve, brings the train into Dolgoch, which means "Red Meadow". The train waters here from a veritable museum piece — an old wooden tank fed from a barrel sunk in a stream higher up the mountain. It must be one of the world's most beautiful stations — buildings of weathered stone set in a blaze of rhododendrons, yellow gorse (a kind of Scotch broom), primroses and purple foxgloves. The Dolgoch estate was presented to the people of Towyn and the visitor is free to wander the mountain paths and inspect the three waterfalls.

Rowland Emmet, creator of the comic railway, "Far Tottering and Oyster Creek", watches the finer points of railroading on a Talyllyn train in the Welsh mountains. Made famous by cartoons in London's *Punch,* the "Far Twittering" line is described in Chapter XVIII.

Interior of the Talyllyn Railway shops at Pendre (West end). This old building has seen repairs to motive power and rolling stock since the line opened in 1865. Coaching stock, seen on the right, has been augmented by two Glyn Valley tramway coaches which were found in a field. The fact they had been used as hen houses did not prevent their complete restoration to such a state of perfection that there is a small supplementary fare of one shilling (about 20 cents) for riding in them.

Members of the Talyllyn Railway Preservation Society at work in the Hendy Cut, as seen from Hendy Bridge. Complete re-laying of the track was necessary for the seven-mile line in Wales.

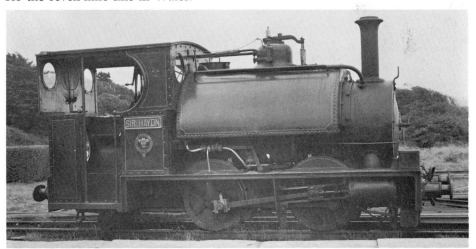

No. 3 *Sir Haydn*, which came from the Corris Railway. She was built in 1878 and took the place of the original engines *Talyllyn* and *Dolgoch* when they were sent to be completely overhauled at Midland factories.

Paul Popper

An idyllic scene on the slopes of Cader Idris mountain where, it is said, a man forced to stay overnight on the fog-bound heights, wakes either a bard (perhaps like Dylan Thomas) or a madman . . . The locomotive is No. 6 *Douglas* and the passengers have taken their choice of closed or open rolling stock.

The woodland scales the mountain beyond Dolgoch as far as Quarry Siding and then the Talyllyn Railway is out in the wildness of rock and scree and the wind of high altitudes. Finally, at the head of the Fathew valley, the line reaches the upper terminal of Abergynolwyn. An extension is planned which will take the little railway over the disused mineral line to the station planned at Nant Gwernol. The cost of restoration will be considerable, and the Society does not propose to embark on the project until the existing sections are without engineering and aesthetic blemish. On this track the railway's first locomotive depot was located.

For the opening of the Talyllyn Railway in 1865, two locomotives were ordered from Fletcher, Jennings and Co. of Whitehaven, Cumberland. First to be delivered was the 0-4-0 saddle tank engine No. 1 *Talyllyn*. Owing to excessive overhang at the rear, the engine was condemned as unstable and the frames were lengthened and a pair of fixed trailing wheels added. Later, she was rebuilt with new frames. No. 1 was soon followed by her sister, the 0-4-0 well tank engine No. 2 *Dolgoch*. In this locomotive the driving axle is mounted behind the firebox, the Allan straight link motion being operated by eccentrics on the leading axle. The object of this unusual design was to secure the adhesive advantage of the 0-4-0 wheel arrangement without the disadvantage of excessive overhang.

No. 1 has 28-inch coupled wheels, while those of No. 2 are 30 inches in diameter. There are also slight differences between the two boilers, but despite their very different appearance, the leading dimensions are similar:

     Cylinders: 8 in. x 16 in.
     Grate area: 2.88 sq. ft.
     Total heating surface: 113.88 sq. ft.
     Weight in working order: approximately 8 tons.

For no less than 86 years, these two locomotives were wholly responsible for the traffic and neither was ever reboilered or extensively rebuilt, an astonishing record of longevity. When the Preservation Society took over in 1951, the *Talyllyn* had been out of service for some years. The sisters soon got to be known by members as "The Old Ladies" and a special correspondent of the London *Times*, visiting the Towyn Pendre shops in 1951, wrote of *Talyllyn* suffering from "bulges in the firebox and unwelcome daylight in the smokebox". In another locomotive shed, he saw "her altered and overhauled sister, *Dolgoch*, in fairly good shape, if one ignores her drooping buffers". In fact she continued to work until 1954, when she was withdrawn for complete

The hedges of the Talyllyn line were planted to keep sheep from straying onto the track. But when Farmer Jones forgets to shut the gate the Welsh cattle find the grass much greener along the right of way. No. 2 *Dolgoch* waits patiently for the "highball" to proceed.

Paul Popper

Lady Northesk, wife of the Talyllyn Railway Preservation Society's president, Lord Northesk, is a regular rider on the little open cars of this slim-gauge pike in North Wales. Her two dachshunds never miss a chance of a ride.

overhaul. A boiler fund has been launched by members and *Dolgoch* is expected to be back in service in 1959.

Talyllyn is already back in service after a long overhaul in a Midland locomotive works and shares the load with two ex-Corris Railway engines. Both of the latter are 0-4-2 saddle tanks. They were numbered 3 and 4 on the Corris and by coincidence they retain the same numbers in the *Talyllyn's* stud. On entering their new service they were named *Sir Haydn* and *Edward Thomas*. Sir Haydn was of course the chief shareholder of the old company and Edward Thomas has been active in the practical administration of the railway for 60 years. He is now a director of the Company.

Particulars of the two locomotives are as follows:

No. 3 *Sir Haydn*

    Built: Hughes Engine Co., Loughborough, 1878.
    Valve gear: Inside Stephenson.
    Coupled wheels, diameter: 2 ft. 6 in.
    Working pressure: 135 lbs. (temporarily reduced from 160 lbs.).
    Cylinders: 7 in. by 12 in.
    Grate area: 3.1 sq. ft.
    Total heating surface: 156.3 sq. ft.
    Tractive effort at 85 percent w.p.: 2,280 lb.
    Weight: Nine tons.

No. 4 *Edward Thomas*

    Built: Kerr Stuart & Co., Stoke on Trent, 1921 (rebuilt,
        Hunslet Engine Co., 1951-2).
    Valve gear: Outside, modified Hackworth.
    Coupled wheels, diameter: 2 ft.
    Working pressure: 160 lbs.
    Cylinders: 7 in. by 12 in.
    Grate area: 4 sq. ft.
    Total heating surface: 126 sq. ft.
    Tractive effort at 85 percent w.p.: 3,332 lb..
    Weight: 8 tons.

Whereas the original Talyllyn locomotives have screw brakes only, No. 4 is fitted with a steam brake and No. 3 has vacuum brakes.

The latest addition to the Company's stud is No. 6 *Douglas* which was presented to the railway by Abelson & Co. (Engineers) Ltd., Birmingham, in April, 1953. After being overhauled and converted from 2 ft. to 2 ft. 3 in. gauge at the expense of members of the Society, this little engine, an 0-4-0 well tank, went into service during the summer of 1954. Leading dimensions are:

This is the upper terminal at Abergynolwyn at the head of the Afon Fathew valley. An extension is planned from this point over a disused mineral line to Nant Gwernal.

John Adams

Talyllyn Society members are straining every nerve to complete an extension of the line to a new terminal at Nant Gwernal in time for the celebrations of the Centennial in 1965. But more "amateur railroaders" are needed from all over the world if such a project is to be completed in time. Here are some muscular members which include lawyers, architects, clergymen.

Built: Andrew Barclay & Co., Kilmarnock, 1918.
Valve gear: Outside Walschaerts.
Coupled wheels, diameter: 1 ft. 10 in.
Working pressure: 150 lbs.
Cylinders: 6¾ in. by 10¾ in.
Total heating surface: 136 sq. ft.
Tractive effort at 85 percent w.p.: 2,828 lb.
Weight: 7 tons.

In addition to the live steamers, the roster includes a Ruston diesel locomotive, a Mercury Tractor and a light gasoline driven trolley which is of great assistance to the track maintenance staff in patrolling the line and carrying out minor repairs.

For the commencement of passenger service in 1866, four 4-wheeled coaches and one 4-wheeled brake van were ordered. The first to be delivered was a rather antique looking vehicle but was followed by three more coaches of more modern appearance, one of which was a first class car and the other a composite first and third class vehicle. Unlike the Festiniog, the Talyllyn has now abolished first class fares, and the antimacassars of the "Little Centenarian" find no place in the scheme of things.

All this rolling stock is still in regular use, so that its record of continuous service is as noteworthy as that of the two original Talyllyn locomotives. The need for new passenger equipment, in view of the increasing flood of summer visitors, has become very pressing. First additions were open four-wheelers acquired through the generosity of the Penrhyn Quarry Company. They were used for quarrymen's trains on the 2 ft. gauge line between Bethesda and Port Penrhyn. Additional vehicles of the same design have since been built in the Company's own shops.

In 1957, Society members rescued from a garden at Chirk a Glyn Valley tramway coach which has now been beautifully restored and is in service. A second Glyn Valley tramway coach has also been acquired and a double truck car from the Corris Railway. With the exception of the Glyn Valley vehicles all the rolling stock for passengers carries the Company's attractive crest of the Prince of Wales' feathers, linking the Talyllyn, however indirectly, to Prince Charles, Queen Elizabeth's son, who now that he is Prince of Wales, will be presented to the Welsh people in ancient Caernarvon Castle. Both the Glyn Valley coaches are now in service, fitted up with luxurious seats and a supplementary fare is charged for travel on them.

No. 4 *Edward Thomas*, watering from a veritable museum piece at Dolgoch. The old wooden tank on the little tower is fed from a barrel sunk in a mountain stream. Almost as much water escapes from the decrepit hose as enters the engine's tanks.

The track, as originally laid in 1865, consisted of flat-bottomed iron rails weighing 44 lbs. per yard and in lengths of 21 ft. The ties were laid 3 ft. apart. There were no fish plates at the joints; instead, the two rail ends rested in a common chair where they were held in place by an oak key. In addition to these joint chairs there were two intermediate keyed chairs to each rail length. The rails were secured to the rest of the ties by dog-spikes.

At some little-remembered date the decision was made to fit fish-plates and do away with the old joint chairs, but on a considerable section of the line between Dolgoch and Abergynolwyn this conversion was never carried out. When the Preservation Society assumed responsibility for the little line it was in an appalling state. Rails were worn out and the ties were rotten. The gauge varied as much as three inches and must have provided the bumpiest ride in Britain. Rehabilitation of the track called for the greatest part of the Society's capital outlay and a considerable portion of the work was undertaken by the voluntary labor of members. Together with the help of a small permanent staff in the winter months and assistance from the Territorial Army (equivalent of the National Guard in the United States), the entire main line has been relaid. The replacement rail, which is flat-bottomed spiked direct to the ties, has come from a variety of sources, including the Corris Railway and the old Welsh Highland.

The little Talyllyn used to be worked on the "one engine only in steam" principle; but the widespread publicity and the tremendous growth in passenger traffic has made it necessary to introduce the divisible staff system and to lay the new crossing loops at Brynglas and later at Rhydyronen. To facilitate this new system of working, all stations are now linked by private telephone. A color light "calling on" signal operated from the Wharf station office has been installed in the cut at the approach to the terminal to eliminate the risk of conflicting movements under the bridge at the station approach; but with this exception there are no signals. As an additional safety precaution all main line points are fitted with locks, while at the Wharf and in the yard at Pendre the point levers have been grouped for ease of working.

The passenger rolling stock is not fitted with continuous brakes, but a brake van is always coupled at the rear of "up" trains to prevent any danger of breakaways on the long ascent.

This, then, is the Talyllyn Railway. It is no sentimental attachment to steam. It is not a museum, although the Society has one at Towyn with the avowed objective of gathering together narrow-gauge

The Territorial Army, equivalent of our National Guard, helping with the Talyllyn track-laying as an exercise in railway work. But the main burden of track rehabilitation rested in the capable hands of over two thousand members of the Talyllyn Railway Preservation Society.

No. 3 *Sir Haydn* standing just beyond Abergynolwyn station awaits the arrival of the "up" train from Towyn. *Sir Haydn* commemorates one of the past owners who, rather than let the company go out of existence, maintained a minimum schedule throughout the most difficult years before the Preservation Society members took over.

railway exhibits from all over the British Isles. The line itself is a monument to a dedicated group of people who felt that things other than ancient buildings should be preserved. Moreover, its existence can be justified by the pleasure and relaxation it gives an increasing number of visitors from all over the world. As the *Railway Magazine* says in one of its recent issues: "Let those of us who love small steam locomotives never forget the debt we owe to the small band of enthusiasts who first founded the Talyllyn Railway Preservation Society, for it was by their determination, courage and sheer hard work that the line was saved from extinction and is still with us today giving so much pleasure to so many."

Membership of the Talyllyn Railway Preservation Society costs £1 ($3.00) per annum and full details can be obtained from the Hon. Secretary, P. B. Whitehouse, 344 Lordswood Road, Harborne, Birmingham 17, England. The little railway publishes much literature of interest to railroadians, such as the official guide, colored postcards and calendars, and full details of these can be obtained from R. K. Cope, Publicity Director, "Brynglas", Beckman Road, Pedmore, Stourbridge, Worcestershire, England.

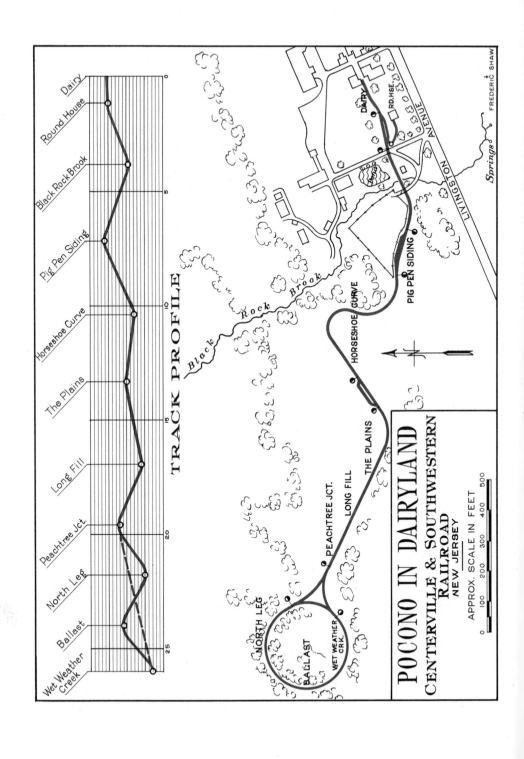

TRACK PROFILE

Dairy
Round House
Black Rock Brook
Pig Pen Siding
Horseshoe Curve
The Plains
Long Fill
Peachtree Jct.
North Leg
Ballast
Wet Weather Creek

POCONO IN DAIRYLAND
CENTERVILLE & SOUTHWESTERN
RAILROAD
NEW JERSEY

APPROX. SCALE IN FEET
0   100   200   300   400   500

FREDERIC SHAW

DAIRY
RD. HSE.
LIVINGSTON AVENUE
Springs
PIG PEN SIDING
HORSESHOE CURVE
THE PLAINS
LONG FILL
PEACHTREE JCT.
NORTH LEG
BALLAST
WET WEATHER CRK.
Black Rock Brook

CHAPTER IX

POCONO IN DAIRYLAND

The Centerville and Southwestern Railroad

AN EDITORIAL WRITER of the London *Times* paraphrased a familiar quotation recently when he said that "today, all too regardful of their doom, the little railways puff." At Roseland, ten miles from Patterson, New Jersey, in a south-westerly direction, is a little line taking no cognizance of awful prognostications. It arose not from economic need as a common carrier but as a gesture of goodwill by a dairyman who wanted to show his appreciation of his customers' patronage over a long period of years.

The Centerville and Southwestern Railroad is a true miniature and is conducted in the same manner as a standard gauge line. It operates on a strict schedule, goes somewhere and comes back—not just around a loop. And it runs through natural scenery whose characteristics lend themselves to the illusion that in all respects the traveler is on a Class I railroad. For a 9⅞₆″ gauge track, this is quite an accomplishment. And the story bears telling.

Before 1879 Roseland was known as Centerville, and Henry Becker, a conscientious, hard working farmer, decided he wanted to expand his business. With a borrowed milkcan, he set out with a light, horse-drawn rig for the communities known as the Oranges to the east of Centerville. He had forty quarts of fresh milk to sell on that first attempt and the older generation can probably recall the methods of the door-to-door milkman. They rang long-handled bells and the housewives came out with pitchers and pails. The milk went in foaming in the golden haze kicked up by the dusty, unpaved roads. Unhygienic? That generation survived. So did Henry Becker despite the sale of only half his milk on that first attempt. In fact, the dairy became one of the most modern in the country and has remained in the family ever since.

In the late 1920's, the idea of building a small railroad came to the Becker family but it was built indoors at half-inch scale. It was a

Edw. T. Francis

The No. 1501 on the turntable after leaving the engine house, ready to move out onto the main for a day's work hauling passengers and bringing happiness to a stream of visitors on the C. & S. W.

Henry Becker

Few junior scale railroads anywhere are more carefully built or maintained than is the track and equipment of the Centerville & Southwestern Railroad at Roseland, New Jersey. Here, a farm crew equipped with air tools maintains the mainline track.

rewarding experience and furnished some of the background for the present miniature railroad system which was started in 1938 with 100 feet of track. Naming the little line presented a problem. It was decided to revive the local town's original name of Centerville as to location and let the general direction of the track supply the second half of the name. Thus emerged the Centerville and Southwestern Railroad.

Building the track was wholly accomplished with the regular farm labor in whatever spare time was available. The years have amply demonstrated that it was expertly constructed and laid. Standard 8-lb. steel T rail was fastened to 3" x 3" wood ties with ¼" x 2" railroad spikes, all ballasted in the approved manner with four inches of crushed rock and cinders on a slightly curved sub-grade top for drainage. Minimum radius for curves in yards and switches is one hundred feet, but main line minimum is twice that. Elevation of the outer rail on curves follows standard practice for radius and speed. All curves begin and end with spirals.

The first year's operation brought to light many technical and practical errors which were remedied prior to the opening of the second season. Before 1949 Peach Tree Junction was the end of the line ⁸⁄₁₀ of a mile from the Centerville station. The junction was the wye where locomotives were turned around for the return journey, and avoided the necessity of a turntable. A loop connecting the ends of the wye was subsequently added to extend the length of the ride.

The most significant addition to the equipment roster of the Centerville and Southwestern occurred in 1940. It was one of the most perfect small scale steam locomotives for passenger hauling in the United States, a "Pocono" type 4-8-4. Many things combined to make the engine unique. In the first instance, it was designed by two of the most distinguished locomotive builder officials in the country. Secondly, the engine is the second ever built to have an all-welded boiler. The credit for No. 1501 goes to Mr. H. B. Ayers, retired president of the famed H. K. Porter Co. of Pittsburgh, Pa., locomotive builders for decades, and to Mr. J. B. Ennis, vice-president of the American Locomotive Company.

The shell of the all-welded boiler is from ⅜" steel plate; the crown sheet of the firebox, the inside wrapper and both tube sheets are from ½" plate. There are both 1½" and ¾" tubes, the former originally accommodating the tubes of a superheater which was later removed as unsuccessful. Tested to 450 pounds per square inch, the operating pressure is 150 lbs. p.s.i., which provides ample safety. To avoid scale

No standard gauge refrigerator car is more perfectly built and equipped than this 2″ scale car. It lacks nothing its giant sister has.

Were it not for the man on the left of the photo, this might be mistaken for a scene along any main line railroad curving off among giant trees. Track is on the loop.

forming inside the boiler nothing but rainwater gathered from the roofs of the farm buildings is used. The locomotive easily hauls 14 fully loaded passenger cars over the line despite grades of 2% and 3%.

The highest speed attainable by this handsome locomotive is still not known as it has never been "let all out." But speeds of 25 miles per hour have been reached and as this represents a scale speed of 150 miles per hour for a standard gauge locomotive the remarkable engineering qualities of No. 1501 may readily be seen. One of the few handicaps rendered by its diminutive size is the firing. Sufficient coal and water are carried in the tender to complete two round trips; but there is so little room in the cab a stop is made at a point on the loop midway of each journey for the engineer to fire up again and maintain sufficient operating steam pressure.

The second piece of motive equipment is the "diesel" locomotive No. 1502. Actually, it is a Model F.C. 86, Waukesha gasoline engine mounted rigidly on a heavy cast iron frame. The motor is connected through an air operated clutch to a twin disc fluid drive. A unique feature about the clutch is the need for at least 70 lbs. air pressure (which is the minimum pressure required before moving a train) before the clutch can be engaged. Any movement of the locomotive before there is sufficient pressure to operate the brakes is thus prevented. And once operating, these air brakes, both on the 1501 and the 1502, can smoothly bring a standard train of eight loaded passenger cars traveling at 12 m.p.h. to a dead stop in 200 feet.

The tractive effort of No. 1502 is 1000 lbs. and the length over-all is 11 ft. 3 ins. Mr. H. B. Ayers must again be given the credit for the design of this sturdy power unit. It was rebuilt in the Centerville's own shops in 1949. The mere mention of the word "shops" raises an interesting point. The round house, which is square, was originally built for the railroad, but with a full panoply of machine tools it was evident that the modern milk business needed machine tools too. Consequently, the machine shop has been used over 90 per cent of the time for the maintenance of dairy and farm machinery.

The rolling stock of the Centerville and Southwestern Railroad would make a story all on its own. The first six cars were designed by Mr. Berthold Audsley and made to look like the older heavyweight Pullmans, at least up to the floor level. They ride smoothly on Pullman-type six wheel trucks. Later, the C&S shops designed and built ten more similar cars except that the under-frame is of all-welded construction and they ride on the newer four-wheel trucks. There are refrigerator cars, ballast cars and a caboose which serves a multiple

Henry Becker

Centerville & Southwestern Railroad, 2 inch scale diesel road engine on the Becker Dairy Farms at Roseland, New Jersey. Diesel type locomotive No. 1502 (4-8-4) on the 9⁷⁄₁₆ inch gauge Centerville & Southwestern Railroad at Roseland, N. J. It is 2″ scale, 11′-3″ long and weighs 5,968 pounds. Powered by Mod. F. C. 86 Waukesha engine.

Henry Becker

A train load of passengers starting around the loop at the west end of the main line.

purpose. Besides being a caboose, it is often used as an extra passenger car and as a maintenance car which carries track tools and, with sides removed, a weed sprayer.

All rolling stock is equipped for automatic air brake operation with clasp-type brakes, reservoir, triple valves, conductor's valve and "glad hand" air hose couplings. The air brakes operate exactly as their full size brothers do: a reduction in train pressure applies the brakes; and, conversely, an increase in air pressure releases the brakes. It may at this juncture be interesting to note that the original duplex, cross-compound air pump on the little steel goliath No. 1501 was a complete flop. Its production of compressed air amounted to a maximum 25 lbs. Sparing no effort or expense, the Centerville reached out hands across the sea to the skills of the late Henry Greenly whose name is writ large across the Romney, Hythe and Dymchurch Light Railway in England. The new pump was built incorporating some Greenly designs and maintains 70 lbs. pressure with ease.

Over the years the popularity of the Centerville and Southwestern Railroad grew beyond all expectations. On operating Saturdays visitors flocked to the farm from far and wide. They still do, from the first Saturday in May to the last Saturday in October. Trains are scheduled from 10:00 a.m. to 5:00 p.m. Memorial Day, the Fourth of July and Labor Day are treated as Saturday operations and extend to 6:00 p.m.

It may be, in the evolutionary process, that one day miniature railroads will be propelled with jet fuel. But on the two-mile round trip on the Centerville, "Pocono" is puffing entirely unregardful of its doom. There is too much nostalgia in the minds of people today—this is proved by the fact that 40 per cent of the people carried by the Centerville are adults—for the live steamer to be a short-term proposition. The visitor can relive the scenes of childhood and forget the scientific arcana of jet propulsion.

Of course, the little line has been of importance to the growth and progress of the basic dairy business. It has built up goodwill which itself is reflected in increased sales of the farm's products. But at the same time the public service element in the Centerville cannot be over-emphasized. The farm employees are part of this. Like the operating staff on the Romney, Hythe and Dymchurch in Kent, England, each man acts as a public relations officer, proud of his product or service and contributing much to the sweet liveableness of life.

Woosung Creek Station. The copper cash in use at that time was so minute that for some tickets 1,200 had to be counted. It involved so much labor that frequently four or five booking clerks had to be employed at both Shanghai and Woosung.

The 2 ft. 6 in.-gauge locomotive *Pioneer* on its arrival in China in 1876. Weighing 26 cwt. empty, it was carried by a skillful arrangement of ropes and bamboos by sixteen men a distance of 3 furlongs without the coolies stopping to draw breath!

CHAPTER X

STEAMBOAT ON SHORE

The Shanghai-Woosung Railway

CHINA'S FIRST NARROW gauge railway owed its existence in some measure to a man with a marked record of success in another Asian country. This man was Sir Macdonald Stephenson who brought the East Indian Railway Company into being in London in 1844 and became its first Agent. After three years of discussions and exchange of notes between the various authorities concerned, the building of the railway from Calcutta to Raniganj was sanctioned by the Board of Directors of the Honourable East India Company as "an experimental measure." Stephenson wrote from India: "Active operations have now at the close of 1850 scarcely commenced. The interval has been occupied with discussions, doubts, objections and their solution and removal."

A veritable mania for railways had invaded Calcutta as early as 1845-46. There was no question that "doubts and objections" were serious, but they were nothing in comparison with the difficulties Sir Macdonald Stephenson was confronted with in the Peking of 1863. The people of China appeared to receive his ideas with enthusiasm, but the hereditary rulers of China had a different viewpoint. They held the doctrine in those days that China was the fountain of all knowledge and advancement; and that any suggestions coming from the West must be, in the nature of things, retrogressive.

Stephenson was very anxious to avoid the extravagances in railway construction that had occurred in other countries; but his proposals were so grandiose for the Chinese that his intentions were misunderstood and his mission failed. Those proposals embraced a scheme for bringing the East Indian Railway terminal at Calcutta into direct communication with Peking!

The trading house of Jardine Matheson had always given cordial support to the various efforts for introducing railways into China. They were firmly of the opinion that the only way to construct a line would be to quietly acquire the land and undertake the whole project under the sole control of themselves and their friends. This they pro-

Offloading rails at Woosung creek for the Shanghai-Woosung Railway in 1876. The little railway, which was nine miles long, aroused the suspicions of the ruling powers from the beginning. However, after the *Pioneer* made its first trip on February 14, 1876, the delight of the Chinese people was unbounded.

ceeded to do in 1872. In that year, Richard C. Rapier of Ransomes & Rapier, Ipswich, ignorant of Jardine Matheson's project, conceived of the idea of sending engines, carriages and rails as a gift to the Emperor of China on the occasion of his majority and marriage. British diplomacy was against this and informed Rapier that gifts, and particularly one of great value, would have been accepted and paraded as tribute. However, Rapier persisted and built at the Waterside Works, Ipswich, England, a locomotive of 22 hundredweight for a two-foot gauge track which more than justified the designer's faith at its trials. It was inspected by two directors of Jardine Matheson's newly formed Shanghai Woosung Road Company and ran on a circular track of only one chain radius, maintaining a speed of 15 m.p.h. and hauling several small wagons loaded with pig iron.

Further trials were conducted on a mile of private tramway at Felixstowe in 1875. The little locomotive, appropriately named *Pioneer,* could haul with ease forty passengers and more. It had cast iron wheels of 18″ diameter and cylinders 4″ in diameter. It was decided to alter the cylinders to 5″ diameter. As it had now been decided to send the locomotive to China, wrought iron wheels and steel tires were fitted and the track gauge widened to 30 inches.

Rapier then busied himself in the matter of providing additional capital for an ambitious passenger service. Estimates were prepared. It was proposed to have a liberal supply of ties, 2500 to the mile; rails, 20 lbs. per yard; two engines of six tons each; one first class, one second and four third class carriages. Eventually the rails were made 26 lbs. per yard and the locomotives weighed 9 tons. A Mr. John Dixon solved the problem of additional finance by offering to accept the contract to make and equip the line for 20,000 pounds in cash and 8,000 pounds in shares.

When the equipment and engineers arrived at Shanghai they discovered that most of the capital of the Company had been eaten up in the purchase of the land. Such purchase for the Shanghai-Woosung Road had been a matter of personal bargain with each owner; and when it is mentioned that in the nine miles of the projected railway there were four hundred different landowners, some idea can be formed of the protracted nature of such negotiations. In many instances ownership consisted in a grave of some relative little valued in life, but highly valued as the right-of-way of a steam locomotive. Besides purchasing the land, it was also necessary to proceed quickly with the cuts and fills to prevent the old owners re-entering and taking a quick crop from it.

Paul Darrell Collection

The little *Pioneer*, her track gauge widened to 30 inches, standing by the first train on opening day, July 1876. Her work was done. She had helped to construct the line and was content to leave the hauling of passengers to her bigger sisters, *Celestial Empire* and *Flowery Land.*

The first project was the building of about fifteen small wooden bridges over the various creeks. So numerous were the watercourses that in addition to the bridges more than twenty stout wooden culverts were constructed. Labor was willing and plentiful. However heavy the equipment to be carried, its carriage from place to place was only a matter of skillful arrangement of bamboos and ropes. The *Pioneer* itself was carried by sixteen men a distance of three-eighths of a mile without stopping to draw breath!

On February 14, 1876, the *Pioneer* made its first trip on three quarters of a mile of track. The news was telegraphed to England: "Engine ran today. Chinese delighted."

This initial success was viewed with alarm by the hereditary ruler of Shanghai, known as the Taotai. He was so pressing in his demand for suspension of the line that a compromise was agreed to: operations of the train would be discontinued for one month but the track-laying would go on. The month expired with no further word from the Chinese Government in Peking so the *Pioneer* resumed her journeys along the little line. National and local interest was thereby quickened, much as public reaction to a book banned in Boston can develop phenomenal sales.

The Shanghai *Times* had this to say on March 31, 1876, as reported by one of its correspondents:

"You will be glad to hear that the construction of the little Woosung railway is progressing, and there are symptoms of withdrawal of opposition on the part of the Chinese officials. It is rumoured that a hint was received by them a few days ago from Pekin to see as little as they could of what was happening, and straws seem to confirm this hint of a change of wind.

"The persecution to which I have before referred of people who had sold certain pieces of land has ceased, and one or two plots which the Mandarins show some reason for wishing to recover are likely to be amicably exchanged; for instance, one which touches the river embankment will be readily exchanged for an adjacent piece a little inland, and the piece on the opposite side of the Woosung Creek, to which I referred a few weeks ago as a cause of trouble, will also be surrendered.

"In the meantime there is no interference with the workmen, who are all country people, and things are progressing rapidly. Several miles of road have been completed and ballasted, and the whole country side is alive with interest. . . ."

About the same time the following notice was inserted in the Shanghai newspapers:

On June 30, 1876, American and European residents were invited to make an inaugural trip for five miles along the Shanghai-Woosung Railway. A contemporary report furnishes the information that short as the journey was, refreshments were served and all officials toasted in the "usual English manner."

"In consequence of the crowds of people who assembled daily to stare at the progress of the Tramway, the Municipal Council very wisely desire that rifle practice at the Butts shall cease for the present. Any accident would not only be regrettable in itself, but in the last degree unfortunate from a political point of view, under the circumstances. If no misfortune happens, and the people are not interfered with, they will gaze their fill, and go home with their curiosity satisfied and a clear idea that railways are not very awful things after all."

As the little railway neared completion, various rumors were circulated as to the intention of the governing powers. A political step was taken by inviting Chinese notables and foreign consuls for an excursion trip. This event was recorded in the North China *Herald* as follows:

"The first railway excursion train in China was run on the May 26, 1876; the excursionists including several ladies, who were accompanied by Admiral Lambert and a party of gentlemen. The train was composed of five ballast trucks, carpeted and otherwise properly furnished for the occasion. The distance traversed extended over about five miles, and the trip was thoroughly enjoyed."

All continued to go well, and no further interference was experienced. The Company's engineers were continually beseiged by applicants for the job of engineer, the argument generally being that the candidate had had experience with steamboats on the river and could equally well handle the "steamboat on shore."

On May 30, 1876, the first permanent locomotive arrived. It was named *Celestial Empire;* and in a few days it was assembled and underwent its trials, putting up a fine performance of 25 m.p.h. Another engine of similar design was named *Flowery Land.* Rolling stock, which arrived with the first engine, consisted of the following:

1 first-class carriage, 15 ft. long, accommodating 16 passengers
2 second-class carriages, 15 ft. long accommodating 18 passengers
4 third-class carriages, 18 ft. long accommodating 96 passengers
12 trucks 10 ft. by 5 ft. by 1 ft. 6 in. weighing empty 25 cwt.

A third locomotive, a 0-6-0T named *Viceroy,* was built but records are incomplete as to whether it was ever delivered.

From experience, it was determined that many trains required third class rolling stock only; and the ratio of accommodations required for the different classes of passenger was one first class to two second-class to eighty third-class.

Paul Darrell Collection

Opening day for the Chinese patrons was July 1, 1876, when great was the jostling, pushing and crowding to find the free seats provided. Two days later regular traffic commenced and six trains were scheduled each way.

July 1, 1876 was declared official opening day and a preview was provided the day before for European residents of the area. About 200 took the ride and pronounced it a great success. On opening day the Chinese were invited to ride free and great was the scramble for places. When traffic started on July 3 the directors celebrated the occasion by a dinner and the dispatch of a wire to London for a further set of coaches.

Six trains ran each day from 7:00 A.M. to 6:00 P.M. and the third-class coaches were always jampacked. Tickets were printed in English on one side and Chinese on the other. The little line seemed destined to succeed like the first railway in India twenty years previously. There were, however, vast differences between Indian and Chinese politics. Freed from the hand of the John Company, as the Honourable East India Company was called, India was quick to take advantage of improved communications under a stable Indo-British government. China, in 1876, was very much a feudal country. Her hereditary rulers, feeling their power usurped, were quick to seize on incidents they could twist to advantage. On August 3 a lunatic committed suicide under the train. The case was reported to the Taotai of Shanghai who expressed the belief that there were at least five hundred men anxious to commit suicide on the Shanghai-Woosung line! In fact, the suicide aggravated an issue that was vexing both Chinese and British, the murder of an Englishman named Margery. The railway was ordered to cease operation by a British diplomat who felt that the Chinese would accept non-operation as a gesture of goodwill while redress was sought.

Nothing could have been worse. The Chinese pressed their advantage and succeeded in jockeying the promoters of the railway into selling it. The terms made were that the provincial government purchased the line at a price corresponding with its cost; that the money should be paid in three half-yearly payments; and that until the purchase price was completed the Company should continue to operate it.

The Chinese soon became very adept as fitters, firemen, brakemen and platelayers. More than half the stock was held by Chinese nationals. The trains continued to operate profitably and often attained revenue of 27 pounds per mile per week.

It was at first hoped that the line would be continued after the Chinese had completed their purchase, but months passed without definite arrangements, and hopes gradually faded. Despite the strongest representations made by British consular officials, the little line

Engine and carriage sheds at Shanghai. Seen in the photograph are the two permanent locomotives, the 0-6-0T *Celestial Empire* and *Flowery Land.*

seemed doomed to an uncertain future. It may be of interest to note at this point that in view of the success of the Shanghai-Woosung Railway, the Governor of Formosa invited the Company's engineer, Gabriel James Morrison, to inspect the terrain with a view to engineering a trans-island railway and using the unwanted road on the mainland as the first section.

Trains continued to run during the Spring and Summer of 1877 without accident or interruption. The time now rapidly approached for giving the railway up, despite the demonstrated need and public acceptance. The value of property had increased, boatmen and hand-cartmen had double employment instead of being thrown out of work, as had first been expected. A petition was presented to the Viceroy from the merchants and people of Shanghai, Kangwan and Woosung for the continuance of the line after handing it over to the Chinese Government on October 21, 1877. All to no avail.

The last installment was paid by the Mandarins on October 20, at 2:00 P.M. and the little railway officially handed over. The last train ran on October 20 from Shanghai at noon and from Woosung at 1:00 P.M. The train was the longest and heaviest ever and all along the track great crowds foregathered. A special train was readied for the Mandarins, but it was declined with impassive dignity. They preferred to go in their chairs, the journey taking three hours to Woosung and nobody knows how many hours in returning to Shanghai.

The track was eventually removed and flung into the Yangtse, but was subsequently salvaged. The governor of Formosa was gratified to learn that Morrison's visit was not in vain and that he could avail himself of half the track for the start of the first Formosan railway. What happened to the engines of the Shanghai-Woosung railway is not known, but the other half of the track was shipped back to England and reposed for many years on the roadbed of the three-foot gauge Southwold Light Railway in Suffolk, England.

The first railway in China was probably the first in the world to be completed, worked at a profit for twelve months, and purchased in cold cash for the sole purpose of scrapping it. Only by scrapping the line did the Mandarins feel they could "save face" and maintain their traditional authority. The power and prestige of Jardine Matheson, the greatest trading house in China, was not able to ruffle that authority.

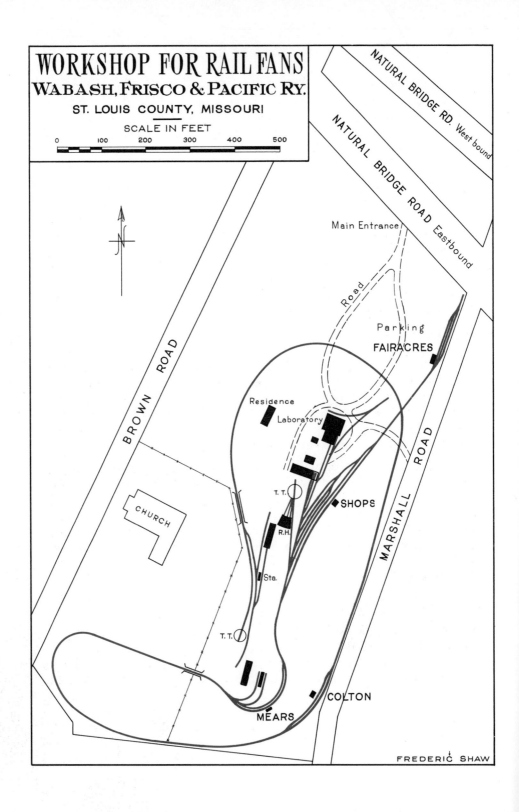

WORKSHOP FOR RAIL FANS
WABASH, FRISCO & PACIFIC RY.
ST. LOUIS COUNTY, MISSOURI

SCALE IN FEET

0   100   200   300   400   500

N

NATURAL BRIDGE RD. West bound

NATURAL BRIDGE ROAD Eastbound

Main Entrance

Road

Parking

FAIRACRES

BROWN ROAD

Residence

Laboratory

MARSHALL ROAD

T. T.

♦ SHOPS

R.H.

CHURCH

Sta.

T. T.

COLTON

MEARS

FREDERIC SHAW

CHAPTER XI

WORKSHOP FOR RAIL FANS

The Wabash, Frisco and Pacific Railroad

THE AMERICAN RAILROADS are trying to tell the people of their present day plight with passenger traffic falling off 40 per cent since the late war. They have been accorded the dubious distinction of being the most over-regulated industry in the country; and although freight revenue has absorbed passenger deficits, the future seems very dark. One thing is certain: public opinion must be rallied behind the railroads for better understanding of their problems and what needs to be done to solve them.

In a very small way, a miniature railroad in St. Louis County, Missouri, is contributing towards this understanding. The object of the group which heads up this little line is to bring together persons interested in the construction and operation of a railway. Participating in all the activities of railroading, the members become more appreciative of a railroad's problems and the many details confronting the management.

The name of this little railway is the Wabash, Frisco & Pacific Association Railroad, approximately a mile long and covering thirty acres of ground on the estate of Wilfred Schade. The system comprises regulation switches and signals, telegraph and telephone lines, machine shop, two station houses, a 25-foot trestle, turntable, tool house and dispatcher's office. Members participate in all phases of railroading: surveying and grading of the right-of-way; draining problems; laying rail; driving spikes; ballasting track; installing switches and signals; operating trains by time table and train order; studying the Book of Rules; designing and building cars; maintaining and improving the steam locomotives; and on a management level, studying the executive phases of railroading, including the purchase and procurement of materials, operations and finance.

Most industries and professions have their workshops and seminars, conducted by experts for the benefit of those interested in

143

W. F. & P. Asso.

Origin of this diminutive 12″ gauge iron colt is in doubt but to its creator should go the plaudits of all railway students for assembling a most attractive locomotive.

Black Star

Every phase of railroad maintenance and operation is engaged in on the W. F. & P. operation. Every "student" railroader must start at the bottom and "work up" to top positions. Here is a scene at the Dispatcher's desk where a youth is learning the intricacies and responsibilities of this critical job.

advancing in their chosen work or avocation. The Wabash, Frisco and Pacific Association Railroad is the first attempt at a railroad workshop.

Spearheading the enterprise, which is a non-profit corporation, is a Pullman man, J. L. "Joe" Christen. He gathered around him other railroad hobbyists. They acquired a 12-inch gauge locomotive and the use of a fine 30-acre estate. This was in 1939. The hobbyists were doctors, design engineers, research chemists, college students, store buyers, farmers and air-conditioning engineers. The first official spike was driven on December 23, 1939, and the original plan for trackage finished on December 8, 1940. In little less than a year, 1982 feet of track were laid requiring 2000 ties and 7000 spikes. As a tribute to the three railroads which have home offices in St. Louis the name of Wabash, Frisco & Pacific Association was chosen. Application was made in 1940 for incorporation as a non-profit organization with a Board of Governors composed of seven members, including the president, all of whom are elected by the membership.

The first engine, No. 171, was a 4-4-0 type with 130 pounds of steam pressure and a tender capacity of 90 pounds of coal and 20 gallons of water. Later, a second engine, No. 180, was acquired. It operates under a head of 140 pounds of steam, and its tender has a capacity of 150 pounds of coal and 23 gallons of water. A third engine, No. 400, has been in operation since December 1949. It is a 4-6-2 Pacific with steam pressure of 200 pounds, a tender capacity of 185 pounds of coal and 30 gallons of water. These steam bantams of the high iron were completely overhauled in the WF&P shops. No. 400 was built in England. All engines were given air brakes, new tenders being constructed for engines 171 and 180. The Pacific was Americanized but retained her plate frame and her 20-spoke drivers as departures from American railroad practice.

Motive power got a big boost when No. 180 received a bigger and better boiler. Working pressure was increased from 140 lbs. to 200 lbs. And additions to the stud are beyond the planning stage. A member, V. A. Schmidt, is building an Atlantic type 4-4-2, rebuilt from a 4-4-0 purchased from the House of David. Mr. Schmidt actually built just about everything from scratch, save the cylinders, valve gear and drive wheels. Other members have dubbed the workmanship "superb." The engine's boiler was built to the Wabash's own drawings by Ott Brothers of Springfield, Illinois. Locomotive dimensions are as follows:

Gauge: 12 inches
Valve gear: Baker

Cliff B. Shirley

Built in England in 1940 of typical British design, this 12″ gauge steam locomotive found its way ultimately to the United States. It had two or three owners before acquisition by W. F. & P. It was sent to the company shops where it was Americanized. The one radical departure from American practice is the plate frame which was left unaltered.

W. F. & P. Asso.

This photo reveals how professionally the amateur owners of the W. F. & P. 12-inch gauge line build their track. Save for switch stand lamps and marker lights on their cars, everything is kept to a rigid scale. Professional railroaders will instantly catch the error of this photo — with the switch closed, the arrow points in the wrong direction.

Fuel: Oil
Drivers: 10¾"
Boiler pressure: 200 lbs.
Cylinders: 2¾" by 4½"

It is anticipated that the new Atlantic will be in service by December, 1958.

Other membership activity includes work on a 4-8-4 which has been under construction for some time. Yet another member purchased three 15-inch-gauge chassis and plans to use two of them to construct a 2-6-6-2 along the lines of the Great Northern behemoths.

The rolling stock is composed of four wooden flat cars, seven all steel flat cars, three all steel gondolas, one aluminum hopper car, one tank car, one observation car, one caboose and fourteen passenger cars. With the exception of the aluminum hopper and the passenger cars, all rolling stock was constructed in the line's own shops by the members themselves. A target has been set for a Pullman or two, so that all phases of railroad operation will be represented in the Association's workshop program.

Most of the W.F. & P.'s rail is 12-pound, some 16-pound being used, and spiked to 4x4x24 inch chemically treated ties, using regulation splice bars and spikes. Apart from the main line, there are an industrial spur, passing sidings and engine house leads, all ballasted with cinders or crushed limestone.

Regularly scheduled trains operate according to Class I railroad practices. A freight train is operated every Sunday morning. In winter, one carload of coal is delivered, according to contract, to the Schade-Paper Laboratory. Four passenger trains are scheduled for Sunday afternoon, No. 9 at 2:30, No. 10 at 2:50, No. 11 at 4:05 and No. 12 at 4:25. But breathes there a railroad with soul so dead that no special excursions are planned? Not the Wabash road! On high days and holidays passenger extras are made up and young and old alike given an insight into what Class I railroading is like on a Lilliputian system. On one day when the St. Louis *Post Dispatch* gave the line a double center page spread in the rotogravure section, a thousand passengers were carried.

A great deal of attention is given to operation, all of which is by timetable, train order and, where applicable, signal operation. Signaling has progressed to the point where the Wabash has a portion of the line equipped with an operating automatic block signal system.

During the winter season 1957-58, two days were experienced when snow-plowing was necessary! On one day there was a foot of

W. F. & P. Asso.

Pacific type (4-6-2) locomotive No. 400 on the Wabash, Frisco & Pacific 12-inch gauge railroad, hauling a load of happy passengers over its well-built main line.

Black Star

A "way freight" out on the main line under command of the "captain" (conductor) setting out units of the freight consist. Switch stand, dwarf signal and the marker lights on the "crummy" are the only adjuncts out of scale.

snow which would have been an equivalent of fifty-five inches on a standard gauge railroad. The snowplow was attached to a flatcar and did fine work clearing the line. What aided the situation was the track layout of the Wabash which is largely on fills and not in cuts.

At the Wabash workshop for rail fans there is a nice balance between students of mature years and the younger generation. Members sometimes start in their high school years and continue with their absorbing interest right through college. It is not uncommon for such students to be elected to the Board of Governors. Once graduating as operating personnel, they must pass examinations based upon the Standard Code of Operating Rules as designed by the Association of American Railroads. Such an examination includes train orders, signals, carrying of proper classification signals and marker lights and standard railroad safety practices. For, whatever a student's specialty, he may be called at any time to man a "work extra" and work the business end of a shovel in maintaining the right-of-way. Admittedly less interesting than "ridin' the rails" as trainmen, the detail for this type of work never lacks enthusiasm.

What makes the Wabash road unique is the workshop's projection of the operation of major railroads into its own miniature railway system. The "faculty" and student body are, in a sense, studying a national problem. By constant practical application of the principles that made railroads successful they cannot fail to advance a few ideas for the betterment of the railroads' lot.

The W.F. & P. has been visited by many top executives of Class I railroads; and they see in this miniature system a community's devotion to the best practices of railroading and a hope for the future. In 1900, 84 per cent of travelers between towns in the United States moved by rail. Today, the figure is 4 per cent for long and short hauls. The workshop is not concerned with national statistics; but it is showing the way to a better understanding of what railroads mean to the country.

The line has not been without its troubles. The school board, which owned the adjoining property, forced the relocation of track and the net abandonment of about 500 feet. But the Wabash road has not missed an operating day since the opening in 1939. The relocation was done by tearing up the track after the last train on Sunday and relaying for operation the next Sunday.

As president of the road and presiding genius of the workshop, Mr. Christen is confident of the future. The operation of live steamers,

W. F. & P. Asso.

Snow is no respecter of persons — nor railroads either. Here, locomotive No. 400 is out on the line pushing a wedge plow ahead to clear the track of accumulated snow.

W. F. & P. Asso.

Another efficient little 12-inch gauge engine on the W. F. & P. line. The chassis, except for the engine truck, looks very much line an early Cagney product.

though an avocation and not a profession, is his lifelong interest. He constructed his first miniature railroad in 1908. In his early school days he was a "nickel an hour" worker in his father's factory and rode the "accommodation" train, now known as the commuter train, between his home in St. Louis and the factory. Prior to starting work with the Pullman Company in 1922, he was shipping clerk and dealt with the handling of railroad merchandise.

His sons, Joseph Jr. and John, have become fully fledged members of the workshop. They are serious young men, representative of a generation not familiar with live steamers on the major railroads but sure nevertheless their efficiency has a lesson for railroaders today. Whether they and their fellow students act as president or the greenest "gandy dancer," they may have something to say about the future of American railroads. They are saying it on the W.F. & P.

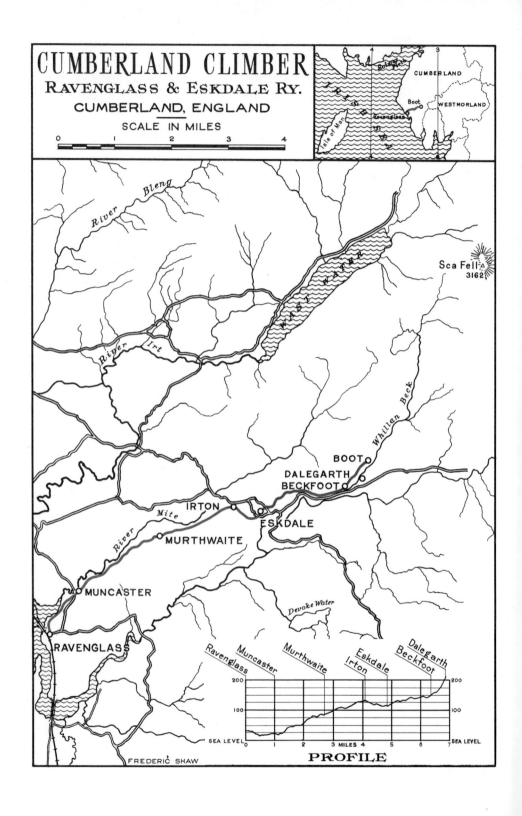

CUMBERLAND CLIMBER
RAVENGLASS & ESKDALE RY.
CUMBERLAND, ENGLAND

SCALE IN MILES

0   1   2   3   4

CUMBERLAND

WESTMORLAND

Isle of Man

Boot

Ravenglass

River Bleng

River Irt

Sca Fell
3162

Whillan Beck

BOOT
DALEGARTH
BECKFOOT

River Mite

IRTON

ESKDALE

River

MURTHWAITE

Devoke Water

MUNCASTER

RAVENGLASS

Ravenglass   Muncaster   Murthwaite   Eskdale   Dalegarth
                                        Irton   Beckfoot

200 — 200
100 — 100
SEA LEVEL
0   1   2   3 MILES 4   5   6   7   SEA LEVEL

FREDERIC SHAW

PROFILE

CHAPTER XII

CUMBERLAND CLIMBER

The Ravenglass and Eskdale Railway

THE TITLE OF "the smallest railway in the world," which belongs to the Ravenglass and Eskdale Railway in Cumberland, England, is a reminder that the British like superlatives too! They are handicapped when it comes to size, as Britain is a tight little island where the traveler can never get farther from the sea than seventy-five miles. Hence the use of the superlatives like the oldest, or the most picturesque, or the smallest!

The line was started in 1915 by three of the "greats" of the miniature railway world and runs through some of the most enchanting country in England's Lake District. W. J. Basset-Lowke, Robert P. Mitchell and Henry Greenly all put their minds and talents to work for the "Ratty," as it is sometimes called, and the little road bears the impress of those talents yet.

The Ravenglass and Eskdale Railway was the second line to use the present track layout. In the third quarter of the Nineteenth Century, the presence and value of hematite iron at Boot, since renamed Dalegarth, secured for the organizers the passage of a bill through Parliament for a 33-inch-gauge railway. The line was opened in 1876. Being in one of the greatest natural recreational areas in Britain, it was soon hauling vacationers in large numbers. Freight grew both ways, as residences were erected in Eskdale and consumer goods tended to balance the shipping of ironstone in the opposite direction. The line failed in 1912, however, the chief cause being the diminishing demand for the ore and the increasing use of basic furnaces. As any railroader knows, good passenger business can never offset a serious loss of freight.

The line remained derelict until 1915 when it was visited by Robert P. Mitchell and W. J. Basset-Lowke. It was a forlorn sight. Weeds and tall grasses had obscured parts of the track; green mosses and lichens were creeping over the gray Cumberland stone of the stations; and sheds and rolling stock were rotting. Just two weeks later the "rescue" work was under way. The British move fast when

Henry Buck

The entire assembly of motive power on the Ravenglass & Eskdale Ry. On the left the *River Esk,* in the middle, *River Ir*t and on the right the 0-4-4 tractor propelled by a Ford petrol engine. It is not presently in service.

Henry Buck

A down train just arrived at Ravenglass, its passengers unloaded. It is about to be uncoupled to move onto the turn table preparatory to a return to the upper end of the seven-mile line. The locomotive is the *River Esk* 2-8-2.

a miniature railway is in peril! Narrow Gauge Railways, Ltd. was formed and the rail relaid on the old track-bed to 15-inch-gauge.

The first unit of motive power was the Atlantic type *Sanspareil* designed by Henry Greenly and originally built by Basset-Lowke for the Geneva Miniature Railway in 1912. The general design was an improvement of Greenly's first 15-inch-gauge Atlantic built in 1905 for the Rhyl Miniature Railway in North Wales. The new Atlantic had a tractive force of 680 lbs., as against the 380 lbs. of the older type. Despite Mr. Greenly's confidence in his own locomotives he did admit some doubt as to the over-all performance of the *Sanspareil* on the severe grades of the Ravenglass line.

The completion of the railway was achieved despite the almost insuperable difficulties posed for private enterprise during World War I. The *Sanspareil* proved more than equal to the heavy work of hauling passengers, coal and consumer goods and quarried stone. The changes of grade are too numerous to be given in a small diagram, but on the way to Irton Road, where the scenery is of the wildest character, some of the stiffest are 2.85%, 2.50% and 1.80%. The terminal at Dalegarth, seven miles distant from Ravenglass, is 207 feet above sea level; and it has been computed that the work involved in lifting an average train to the summit represents an expenditure of 30% to 50% more power than would be required to haul the same loads over a level track.

The *Sanspareil* was followed by the Pacific type *Colossus*, built for Captain Howey of the Romney line for his own private estate, and then by the Pacific type *Sir Aubrey Brocklebank*. Both these Pacifics were designed by Mr. Greenly and built by Basset-Lowke of Northampton. The heating surface of the Greenly designed miniatures affords an interesting comparison. *Little Giant*, which was the motive power built for the Rhyl Miniature Railway in 1905, had a heating surface of 5,000 sq. ins.; that of the *Sanspareil* 11,000 sq. ins.; and that of *Sir Aubrey Brocklebank* 12,034 sq. ins. The dimensions of the little express engines, many of which were common to the Atlantic *Sanspareil* and both Pacifics, were as follows:

Cylinders:	4-1/8-in. bore by 6-3/4-in. stroke
Valves:	Bronze slide type on the top of cylinders
Eccentrics:	Solid with the axles
Stephenson's link motion (indirect) Steam ports:	3/8-in. by 2-3/4-in., exhaust 3/4-in.
Coupled wheels:	20-in. diameter on tread

Sturdy *River Esk* 2-8-2 of the Ravenglass & Eskdale Railway of Cumberland, built in 1923 by Davey, Paxman & Co.

No, a cloud is not pulling this full load of sight-seers up into the enchanting hills. But this fine photo could be mistaken for a black and white print of an oil painting. Its composition would excite any artist.

Bogie (truck) wheels: 9-3/8-in. diameter on tread
Trailing wheels: 10-1/4-in. diameter on tread
Axles, coupled: 2-1/16-in. diameter
Boiler barrel: 19-3/8-in. diameter
Length between tube plates: 4-ft. 3-1/2-in. for Atlantics;
                               5-ft. 11-1/4-in. for Pacifics
Total wheel base: 7-ft. 0-3/4-in. for Atlantics;
                               8-ft. 5-3/8-in. for Pacifics
Width over footplates: 2-ft. 5-1/4-in.

In the early days of operation the Ravenglass and Eskdale Railway acquired three locomotives with a most interesting history which were built in the last quarter of the Nineteenth Century. They were named *Katie*, *Ella* and *Muriel* and came from Sir Arthur Heywood's private railway at Duffield Bank, Derby. Sir Arthur was the first man to prove, at least to his own satisfaction, that steam-hauled miniature railways could be of even narrower gauge than the Festiniog. He built, at Duffield Bank between the years 1874 and 1881, a 15-inch-gauge system of considerable proportions. In the approximately one mile of length there were three tunnels, two bridges and a trestle 91 feet long and 20 feet high. The line included six stations, at three of which were sheds for rolling stock.

The track consisted of 14 lb. rails spiked to elm and Spanish chestnut ties. The rails were subsequently relaid at various weights, 14 lb., 18 lb., and 22 lb. per yard; and with the proper spacing of ties, the track was found to be capable of supporting 25 cwt. per axle. The final stage of track laying was completed when a cast iron tie in which the chairs were integrally cast and weighed 28 lb. was perfected. There is no question that the Duffield Bank railway was the precursor of the British 15-inch-gauge miniature lines.

The rolling stock that the Ravenglass and Eskdale Railway took over from Duffield Bank presented no problem. There were originally eight double-truck covered coaches, four double-truck open coaches, a number of freight wagons and a "Heywood" sleeping car, well appointed, which the Ravenglass staff used as night quarters! But the little engines gave Mr. Greenly what is known in the vernacular as a bad time. They burnt four times as much coal as his express engines. Well do the engineers of the time remember *Katie* who was prone to stopping on the severe grades; and while the train staff habitually extolled the virtues of the wild wonderland of dale and mountain to passengers, the engineer would be having a hectic time raising steam pressure!

Henry Buck

The *River Esk* on the turntable about ready to move off and couple onto its passenger consist for a return journey up the hills to Boot, end of the line.

Henry Buck

An excellent close-up of the rod work on the left side of 15-inch gauge locomotive *River Irt*. This engine has outside frames which substantially widens it but lowers the center of gravity.

The next locomotive to enter the service of the smallest railway in the world was a Mikado type freight, named *River Esk*. She was built at Colchester by Davey, Paxman & Co. to Mr. Greenly's design and was the first 2-8-2 type motive power unit to appear on any British railway. Eqiupment included a patent poppet valve and valve gear. The drivers were 17½-in. diameter with steam pressure of 180 lb. and tractive effort of 2,000 lb. The *River Esk* was rebuilt by the Yorkshire Engine Company under the Poultney patent as a 2-8-2+0-8-0 (the 0-8-0 denoting the two-cylinder steam tender). As rebuilt, she was not an unqualified success, and in 1934 reverted to her original design in which guise she appears to this very day. The steam chassis of the tender, however, is stored in a shed for possible future use.

The 0-8-0T *Muriel* from the Heywood stable had her frame lengthened and a trailing axle provided. The old boiler was replaced with a larger one having scale mountings, and a cab fitted, while at the same time the tanks were removed. Equipped with a tender, the locomotive returned to service as the *River Irt*. It is a far call from the Duffield Park line of 1894 to the busy little Ravenglass railway today, but the *River Irt*, resplendent in new paint, has made it!

The "Ratty" today is just as important an institution to British miniature railroaders, particularly Cumbrians, as it ever was. A very high proportion of people living in the Lake District of Westmoreland and Cumberland take a trip along its steam trails at least once a year. Churches, schools and clubs in the locality also plan annual outings and pray for good weather. The weather can make the difference for the little railway between a profit or a loss for the season. But good weather or not, the imperishable qualities of the countryside within a stone's throw, so to speak, of the haunts of the Lakeland poets— Wordsworth, Coleridge and Southey—provide a stronger lure than mere sunshine. The Eskdale district is rich in historical ruins and archaeological remains. The lover of antiquarian lore can revel to his heart's content in reconstructing for himself the pre-Roman times when the Druids practiced their mysterious rites in the temple which remains in an excellent state of preservation not far from Ravenglass. The Romans established a fine port at this western terminal and great military earthworks at Hardknott, farther inland. In fact, there is evidence that during the building of Hadrian's Wall, the barrier built to keep out the bellicose Picts and Scots, Ravenglass was the port of entry for artisans and materials. The remains of Roman occupation may still be seen in the ruins of a villa located in the grounds of Muncaster Castle, one and a half miles from Ravenglass.

Henry Buck

Locomotive *River Esk* entering Ravenglass, seaside terminus of the line. Note that passengers are seated in open coaches, affording the best view of the enchanting countryside — with plenty of fresh air.

Henry Buck

Locomotive *River Esk* on the left and *River Irt* on the right. Note the difference in widths of the two engines. The *Esk* has the conventional plate inside frames while the *Irt* has outside frames.

From the earliest days of operation rolling stock has consisted of both open cars and covered 12-seater coaches. Most people risk the weather and elect to ride as close to nature as possible! A correspondent, Mr. C. F. Moysey of Torquay, writing to the London *Times* in August 1957, spoke of a "delightful and amusing ride" and the fact that "it was quite possible to pick long-stalked flowers from the adjoining banks while the train was in motion without leaving one's seat." Skirting the great green fells, or threading the valleys, or moving through the woods whose floors are covered with brake-fern and flowers, or listening to the ghylls (waterfalls) which feed the calm waters of the lakes—all these things are the passenger's for the price of a 50 cent round trip ticket.

There is no signaling system and it is seldom that trains pass one another en route. On busy days in summer trains are worked one way at intervals, congregating at Dalegarth and then returning, as many as three complete trains, one after another at safe intervals. The track has been maintained all these years in excellent condition, most of the ties being cut down from the standard gauges. All station buildings were painted in 1957. The engine shed at Ravenglass, built for the original 33-inch-gauge line over eighty years ago, is still in use. The Cumbrians build well in their local gray stone; and if a guess may be hazarded, the shed will be standing eighty years from now.

A curious feature of the locomotives is that they have no brakes. Neither do the passenger coaches. To brake, the engines are reversed. And many of the coaches have no springs. No brakes, no springs—but what enchantment this "Cumberland Climber" affords! On what other line can the passenger pick wild flowers from a moving railway coach?

That the "Ratty" may go the way of the Festiniog and Talyllyn is foreshadowed in a leading article published in *The Whitehaven News* under the dateline September 4, 1958:

PRICED AT £22,500
"RATTY" FOR SALE

"The Ravenglass and Eskdale Narrow Gauge Railway, locally known as the "Ratty," is this week being offered for sale as a going concern for an inclusive price of £22,500 [$63,000]. Its future will be viewed with concern by all who love Eskdale and all devotees of miniature railways. Already a move is afoot to interest local people in the railway and secure its continuation as a private railway in its entirety. . . ."

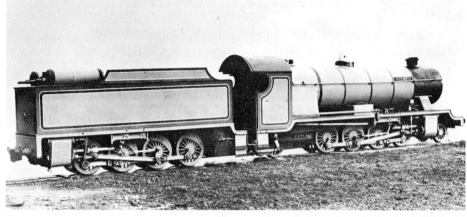

Ravenglass & Eskdale Railway locomotive *River Esk* just out of the shops after being equipped at Yorkshire Engine Co. shops with a steam tender in the year 1928. It operated, not too satisfactorily, in this manner until 1934, when the steam tender was removed and a standard double-bogie tender substituted. This is the sole example extant of so small a locomotive ever having been thus equipped. The tender chassis is stored at Ravenglass and may one day be a part of another, conventional locomotive.

The 0-8-0 tender chassis of the locomotive *River Esk*, stored in the engine shed at Ravenglass against the day it may be given a new lease on life under the boiler of a new locomotive. It is difficult to photograph.

After tracing the history of the little railway, the leading article, quoting from a statement issued by the Directors of Keswick Granite Co. Ltd., owners of the line, reported:

"Since taking the railway over, the Keswick Granite Co. Ltd. have carried out many improvements to the 7½-mile permanent way, fences and buildings. A shop has been erected at Ravenglass, and a cafe at Dalegarth is being successfully run by the Company.

"The rolling stock has been increased considerably and a new model diesel locomotive is at present being built.

"The Directors, however, have decided that the miniature railway should be run independently of the quarrying business, which is the sole interest of the Keswick Granite Co. Ltd., and they hope that a buyer or buyers will be found to take over and develop further this unique undertaking which attracts large numbers to the County every year, and gives pleasure to thousands of those living in it."

Is it too much to hope that enough miniature railway enthusiasts, not only locally in Cumberland but also in all other countries where little live steamers puff, will band themselves together and preserve "this unique undertaking" as the Festiniog and Talyllyn Preservation Societies have done with their own lines?

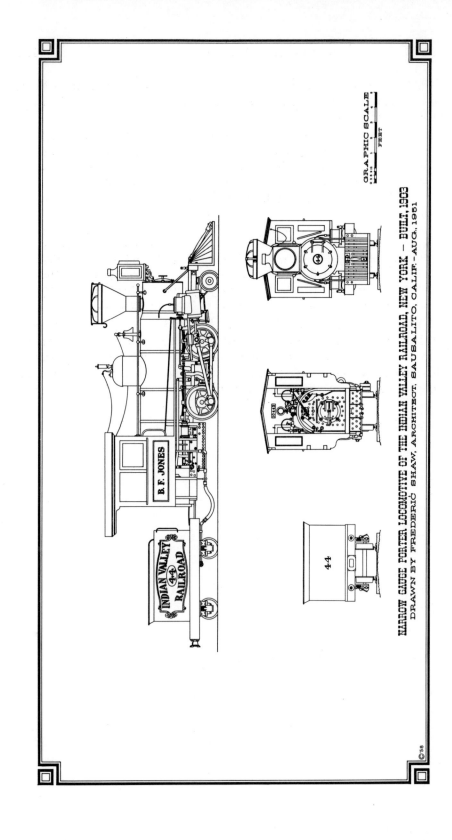

NARROW GAUGE PORTER LOCOMOTIVE OF THE INDIAN VALLEY RAILROAD, NEW YORK — BUILT, 1903

DRAWN BY FREDERIC SHAW, ARCHITECT, SAUSALITO, CALIF.-AUG. 1951

GRAPHIC SCALE

FEET

B. F. JONES

INDIAN VALLEY
4-4
RAILROAD

44

©56

CHAPTER XIII

AN INDIAN VALLEY LINE

William Willock's "Indian Valley Railroad"

THE EXPRESSION "INDIAN VALLEY" is peculiarly American in origin, although the season, Indian summer, is known in various parts of the world. It is a period of calm repose after the heat of the year's prime; and the railroader has adapted the sentiment to a railroad of peaceful perfection which he builds somewhere in his own "Indian Valley."

The country estates of many railroad enthusiasts harbor an individual Indian Valley. One such line exists on Long Island, New York, at the home of William W. Willock, Jr., typifying the ideal. And it started some years ago when he was browsing around a local blacksmith's shop. . . .

Mr. Willock unearthed a quantity of small-gauge steel track. It was 12-lb. rail welded to steel ties in 7½-inch-gauge. Immediately there arose before his eyes the vision of an Indian Valley railroad of his own. He struck a bargain with the blacksmith and bought the lot. Carting the stuff home, he broke out his acetylene torch and separated rails from ties. He next had oak ties fashioned at a local sawmill to the dimensions of 4x6x36 in. They were treated with creosote. The newly acquired rails were then spiked to them for a track gauge of 2 feet.

The original 12-lb. rail proved too light for the motive power and rolling stock Mr. Willock subsequently purchased. The track, so far as completed, was replaced in 1950 with 25-lb. rail.

The 2-foot-gauge was dictated by the ready availability of several brickyard cars. Most of us, in the halcyon days of boyhood, have played with brickyard cars and have experienced their mulish tendencies. The French have an excellent expression little understood in Anglo-Saxondom. They do things *"pour le sport,"* which means, "let's try anything once and to heck with the consequences." French schoolboys have been known to run "dinky" engines on to the main line just to see if the *rapide,* just then about due, could stop in time. If this narrative appears to be getting discursive, it is because there is a note

165

Still lacking the projected ornamental headlight brackets and running boards, the No. 44 is as trim a little locomotive as one could wish. Its owner did all the work of rebuilding.

William W. Willock's 2-foot gauge 0-4-0 Davenport locomotive on the trestle on Mr. Willock's Long Island estate. The gasoline locomotive may be seen below.

The rebuilt Locomotive No. 16 of the Indian Valley R. R. all slicked up with new parts and a new paint job. The Davenport Locomotive Works built the engine originally and reboilered it on its way east to the new owner. The track gauge is 2 feet.

What an unpromising mess the above industrial engine is! Few even of the most ardent locomotive fans would glance twice at this junky-looking engine. But, the man with imagination and mechanical skill sees through the grime and knocked-up appendages and envisions a trim little kettle born of this heap. This is the Willock No. 44 as its owner bought it.

of recklessness in all experimentation with building miniature railroads; and Willock, after the discovery that the brickyard cars would not negotiate the curves of his line, set about looking for a "dinky" locomotive, the kind contractors once used for earth-moving projects.

He temporarily turned himself into a mail-order house and broadcast inquiries for small railroad equipment to junkies and railroad equipment brokers. Two prospects eventually came to light. One was a much-too-heavy Davenport weighing 18 tons. The other was a Porter owned by a steel plant in Ohio. Willock, like the French schoolboys, was in a reckless mood. He bought the Porter sight unseen.

The engine was a sorry mess when it arrived at Indian Valley. The new owner's recklessness persisted. The old Porter was about to fall victim to major surgery. Off came the saddle tank and the cumbersome steel cab. The unusually high steam dome suffered a partial amputation to reduce its altitude. Other modifications were performed in the Indian Valley workshops. A shapely new hood for the altered steam dome was fashioned; a more conventional wood cab was built; and a new boiler jacket was wrapped around new boiler lagging. The smokestack was inadequate and too far removed from the Victorian appearance the owner sought. An inquiry directed to the original builder of the Porter, elicited the information that a new diamond stack would cost half the national debt. Another plan must be devised.

Fortunately, the conical smoke-hood of an old vertical boiler was at hand, which seemed to fit the design Willock had in mind for a balloon stack. He provided the necessary base, top ring and spark screen to amplify the cone and make the well-proportioned stack shown in our photos. But, the engine needed a headlight; and it was some time before an old, square headlight was unearthed in a Connecticut antique shop. Ornamental brackets supporting the headlight platform were designed by the author. The cylinder of an old hoisting engine was adapted to make a steambrake.

Other features were needed to transform the dinky into a locomotive worthy of an Indian Valley Line ideal. Two-wheeled trucks were fashioned in the home workshop and applied beneath the front end and also under the cab. A graceful wood pilot, patterned after early-day design, was made and attached. The first piece of motive equipment for the two-foot railroad was beginning to take shape. The tender came next. Willock built a four-wheeled fuel and water carrier without springs and offered a silent prayer it would safely ride the track.

The trial run of the locomotive proved two faults. An unsprung tender is temperamental, and a trailing truck on an ex-dinky doesn't add anything to riding comfort or rail security. Springs were applied to the tender and the trailing truck under the cab lost its job. The end result of all these efforts was the complete redesign and rejuvenation of a locomotive built in 1903 which the builders, the H. K. Porter Company of Pittsburgh, Pennsylvania, would scarcely have recognized. For efficiency and design, it could not have failed to do the company great credit.

The second piece of motive power was a Davenport locomotive built for the same gauge. Willock purchased it from an Idaho mine in 1951. It was a cap-stacked, saddle-tank 0-4-0. On the way east from Idaho, the little engine was detoured to the Davenport works in Iowa and there reboilered. A new saddletank was added, the tires turned and other improvements made. Inspection, however, revealed a considerable amount of shoddy workmanship, and the new owner was forced to drag the engine into his own shop. The badly fitting saddletank was removed and a new, locally built tank installed. It was some time before all the defects of the machine could be remedied.

Mr. Willock then turned his attention to the car problem. There seemed nothing available but small, four-wheeled dump cars in the two-foot-gauge; but a considerable amount of browsing around eventually turned up at the Upper Saddle River RR at Fairlawn, New Jersey, two eight-wheeled, double-truck flat cars. Since their purchase, however, the flats have deteriorated and construction of new cars is proceeding. Wheels and axles are available to build four new cars, together with steel for frames.

In September, 1953, the Indian Valley made its first concession to modernism through the purchase of a 3-ton Vulcan gasoline locomotive, built in 1925 and formerly used by the Foundation Company of Kearney, New Jersey. This little piece of motive equipment has proved useful in track laying operations. The present line meanders through the woods, and includes a sizeable cut and trestle with concrete abutments. The gang of two—Willock and his hired man—was augmented weekends by willing friends. The Vulcan, No. 104, pushed the flat cars laden with rails and tools and ties. Behind the Vulcan came an air compressor mounted on a four-wheel car, this air tool having been powered by a Model A Ford engine. The compressor furnished air for spike driving and tie tamping. Maximum ruling grade on the first section completed was 5% but on the second section not more than 3%.

The backhead of Wm. W. Willock's 2-4-0 No. 44. The number appearing on the cab wall just above the steam gauge is the New York State Boiler Inspection number, since all boilers require state inspection and certification. Compared to the modern steam giant, this backhead is simple indeed.

This Pike of Peaceful Perfection is a long way from completion but as Mr. Willock would be the first to admit, whoever expects to attain perfection in this life? The important thing is to have plans and abide by them. Ballasting, at this writing, is about completed and a real station, fit for any railroader, will soon be fashioned. The hired hand is a carpenter by trade. He is busy with wainscoating in the main hall and fitting out a station agent's office. A telegraph, pot belly stove and benches are projected and messages that only real, dyed-in-the-wool lightning slingers can send and interpret will eventually provide appropriate communication throughout the length of the line. Also on the drawing board, are gallows-frame turntables for each end of the little railway. ("Armstrong" turntable to the initiated.)

The rebuilt Porter No. 44 was sold, with a keen sense of regret, to a Western-type amusement park, and Willock is concentrating presently on maintaining the Davenport. But who can tell what motive power will greet the visitor to Mr. Willock's estate during the coming years?

To start an Indian Valley line in the first instance means the builder works to a high ideal. And in the world of mechanical things some of those ideals are not easy of attainment. The builder can always think of improvements to track bed, rolling stock, stations, signaling and the like. His motive power never quite measures up to "Indian Valley" standards. Therefore, such a line is always in a state of flux and incompletion. Perhaps it is just as well. Ahead, along those shining "Indian Valley" rails and with the bark of the engine's exhaust in his ears, the builder sees "tomorrow" as the day when his ideal will be achieved and that is where he finds his greatest satisfaction.

Builder's photo of the latest 2-foot-gauge Shay locomotive on the transfer table at Lima Locomotive & Machine Works, Lima, Ohio, for the Gilpin R.R.

CHAPTER XIV

MIXED CONSIST

The Gilpin Railroad—
The Silver City, Pinos Altos and Mogollon Railroad—
Thespian's Pike (William Gillette's private railroad)—
The Mount Gretna Narrow Gauge Railroad—
The House of David Railroad

As ONE GREAT metropolitan newspaper has pointed out, each one of us has a little railway forever lurking in the corners of our mind. In many cases it is a train we remember from childhood. But there is virtually no limit to the categories of road we hold in such special affection.

The model railroader has built one for himself. The historian has read and studied a particular road, perhaps long since dismantled but nevertheless deeply etched on his mind and in spirit well worth traveling over again and again. The armchair traveler has read of many and perhaps settled on one whose features attract him—motive power, rolling stock, wayside stations or even time-tables. Who can forget the Hundred of Manhood & Selsey Tramway, afterwards the West Sussex Railway in England, and its time-table, which was intended only to "fix the time before which trams would not start"?

Whatever our choice, they may find the name of our little railway "indelibled" on our hearts when we die, as Christopher Morley said about his "Paoli Local." In this chapter is a "mixed consist"—to use a railroader's term—of little railways. They have been chosen for the good and sufficient reason that the historian, the model railroader or the armchair traveler has considered them notable and worth revisiting.

No story of the little railways of the world would be complete without mention of two slim gauge lines of the pioneer mining era of the West. Their purpose was purely utilitarian and few people, other than small mining communities, ever saw them; but they presented dramatic features to the railroadian and lived a turbulent life all their own.

The first was the Gilpin County Tramway, afterwards the Gilpin Railroad, located in one of the richest counties in mineral wealth in Colorado, indeed in the whole of the United States. The other 2-foot-gauge railroad was the Silver City, Pinos Altos and Mogollon in New Mexico.

Ten cars of ore were about all an engine could handle "coming down the Mountain" on the Silver City Railroad. The engines were fitted with steam brakes, but it was up to the conductor and brakeman to hold the cars by hand. Wrecks were almost of everyday occurrence.

The local stamp milling industry, which included the old New York Mill shown in this picture, arose in Gilpin County, Colorado, from the need to process ore of too low grade to send to the smelter.

Gilpin Railroad

Since the first gold was panned in Gregory Gulch, Gilpin County, in 1859, the claims located in this area produced much of the gold mined in the state; and it was to serve this area and the local stamp milling industry that the Gilpin County Tramway Company was organized by Frederick Kruse. The 3-foot-gauge Colorado Central Railroad served Black Hawk where in 1867 a smelting plant was erected and gave impetus to the stamp milling which treated the ore too low grade to send to the smelter. But transportation was needed to get the ore from the various claims to the stamps located at both Black Hawk and Central City.

The Tramway connected with the Colorado Central at a place whose name was redolent of the Old West—the Hidden Treasure Mine. The mine was located a half mile west of the Company's frame engine house and machine shop at Black Hawk. The road was constructed with little grading and filling and went up hill and down dale on light rail. But as the Company started to make money the track was relaid with 35-pound steel and iron rail of the same weight and conditions generally improved.

For motive power a Shay geared locomotive was purchased from the Lima Locomotive and Machine Works and shipped to the road on August 10, 1887. She was a double truck type with two 7″ x 7″ cylinders, 24-inch drivers and weighed ten tons. In February of the following year another double-truck Shay arrived, slightly heavier than No. 1, having three 7″ x 7″ cylinders and weighing twelve tons. The company subsequently ordered three more Shay geared locomotives; No. 3 arrived in December, 1889, with three 8″ x 8″ cylinders, weighed 31,000 pounds and had a diamond stack; No. 4 arrived in February, 1900 and also had three 8″ x 8″ cylinders but weighed 34,000 pounds; and No. 5 arrived two years later, identical with No. 4 except for weight which was 36,000 pounds.

Rolling stock consisted mainly of double-truck, steel, drop-bottom, hopper-type ore cars, augmented later by double-truck, light weight flats.

In 1904 the Colorado and Southern bought control of the little tramway, in a minor recession, be it added, for discussions were taking place regarding a change of gauge to the 3-foot purchaser. The Gilpin gained a 4-wheel snow plow, a flat car and a caboose, but lost, one year after being taken over, the first two Shays which went to the Silver City, Pinos Altos and Mogollon Railroad.

No. 3 double-truck Shay of the Gilpin County Tramway, built at the Lima Locomotive and Machine Works. She was sold to the Silver City Railroad of New Mexico and took over main line work when her lighter sisters, Nos. 1 and 2, proved inadequate to the task.

The Silver City, Pinos Altos and Mogollon Railroad followed the roof of the continent and possessed some rough grades. The first two Shay-geared engines were not up to this heavy work and were relegated to switching and hauling out the slag pots. Here is No. 1 at Silver City.

In 1906 the Tramway became the Gilpin Railroad Company and by 1910, at the very zenith of its glory, could boast of 10.67 miles of main line.

Silver City, Pinos Altos and Mogollon Railroad

The Silver City 2-footer answered the same need as the Gilpin. Mines were at Pinos Altos and the smelters and concentrators at Silver City, Grant County, New Mexico. The road, in traveling between the mountain of Pinos Altos and Silver City, followed the roof of the continent, for both were located on the Continental Divide, and in 16 miles of main line there were forty-eight trestles of various heights. In addition to the two Gilpin locomotives, the Silver City purchased three other Shays. Nine or ten cars of ore were all that an engine could handle coming down the Mountain, as Pinos Altos was called. They were fitted with steam brakes, but conductor and brakeman had to hold the cars by hand. Wrecks on the road were an everyday occurrence. It was said that engine crews, in view of the derailments and pile-ups, developed special techniques for jumping clear in a hurry. One wreck in 1907 killed a fireman and inspector. A court of enquiry suggested the company equip its trains with air brakes. The line closed in the fall of the year anyway, just ten years before the Gilpin. They were both examples of extremely rugged railroading, with dramatic motive power deserving of inclusion in the 2-footer Hall of Fame.

Thespian's Pike

Part of the tragedy descending upon many interesting garden railroads is that they occasionally fall into the hands of new and completely indifferent owners. The enthusiast for this type of small railroad is usually somewhat dogmatic about who inherits his miniature railroad property; and if, in his lifetime, he disposes of his line and equipment, he usually insists that it go to another of his kind.

The late William Hooker Gillette (1855-1937), famed playwright and actor, had a most interesting eighteen-inch-gauge railroad on his Connecticut estate in the 1930's. It was three miles long. He was inordinately proud of that serpentine pike, with its tunnels through solid rock, bridges and other scenic effects, and he usually gauged the worth of people's friendship by their interest or lack of it in his railroad. Those displaying enthusiasm for his revered hobby were almost certain of a return invitation.

Gillette wrote in his last testament, "It is my hope the Executors . . . will exercise discrimination in carrying out my earnest wish.

Cliff B. Shirley

This odd and completely unorthodox locomotive is one of two built for and operated on the private estate railroad of the famous Shakespearian actor, William Gillette at Hadlyme, Connecticut. It is a 4-2-2 and now operates in an amusement park.

Thomas Norrell

The second diminutive engine, No. 12, built by Baldwin for the Pennsylvania two-foot gauge pike, Mr. Gretna Narrow Gauge, standing on the turntable in front of the ornate engine shed at the lower end of the line.

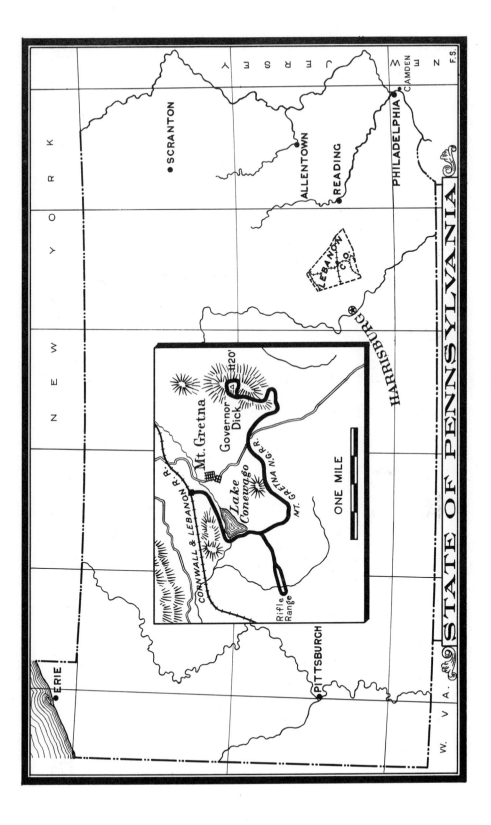

STATE OF PENNSYLVANIA

ERIE

N E W   Y O R K

SCRANTON

ALLENTOWN

READING

PHILADELPHIA

CAMDEN

J E R S E Y

N E W

F.S.

LEBANON CO.

HARRISBURG

Mt. Gretna

Governor's Dick 1120'

CORNWALL & LEBANON R.R.

Lake Conewago

MT. GRETNA N.G.R.R.

Rifle Range

ONE MILE

PITTSBURGH

W.   V   A.

W.   VA.

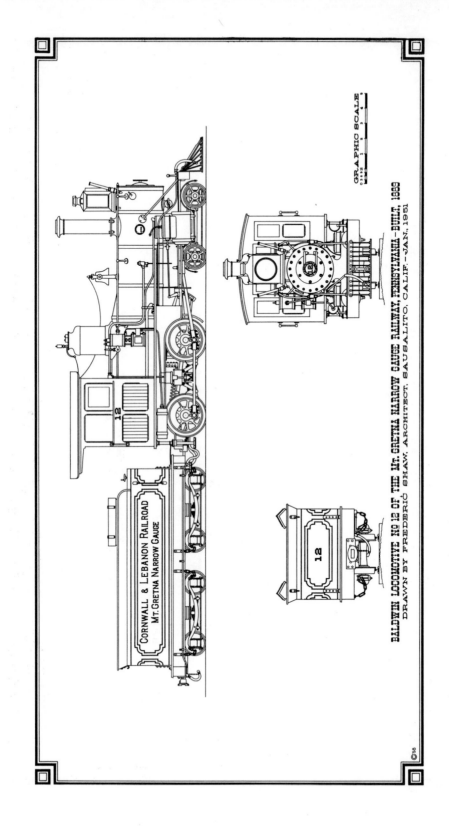

GRAPHIC SCALE

BALDWIN LOCOMOTIVE No 12 OF THE Mt. GRETNA NARROW GAUGE RAILWAY, PENNSYLVANIA-BUILT, 1889

DRAWN BY FREDERIC SHAW, ARCHITECT, SAUSALITO, CALIF.-JAN. 1951

CORNWALL & LEBANON RAILROAD
Mt. GRETNA NARROW GAUGE

12

"I would consider it more than unfortunate for me—should I find myself doomed, after death, to a continued consciousness of the behavior of mankind on this planet—to discover that the stone walls and towers . . . of my home . . . should reveal themselves to me in the possession of some blithering saphead who had no conception of where he is or with what concerned."

William Gillette's pride in his small gauge railroad was indicated by further reference to it in his will as he wrote, ". . . with its bridges, trestles, tunnels through solid rock and stone culverts and underpass, all built in every particular for permanence; my locomotives and cars, constructed on the safest and most efficient mechanical principles . . ." revealed his intense interest in his hobby.

Gillette's estate on the Connecticut River at Hadlyme was named "Seventh Sister," from the southernmost of seven wooded hills along the river between East Haddam and Hadlyme, according to the magazine, "Connecticut Woodlands" of April, 1943.

The eighteen-inch-gauge railroad on the Gillette premises was laid out in the form of an irregular loop approximately three miles in circumference. The three locomotives were of the 4-2-2 type, probably built by some local mechanic and incorporating some of the owner's strange ideas. They were distinctive not alone because of their odd wheel arrangements but also for the fact that they derived their power from two-cylinder steam engines previously extracted from old Stanley steam automobiles. Despite this oddity, they were powerful and efficient, however much they deviated from accepted locomotive mechanical standards.

When the Gillette railroad and equipment was disposed of, two of the locomotives, all of the cars and the track were purchased by Pierce and Norton and set up to run around Lake Compounce near Bristol, Connecticut. The steam power units of the locomotives were removed and well-muffled Dodge auto engines substituted. To carry out the illusion that the locomotives were still "live steamers," a small boiler was provided in each engine to make steam for the whistle! If there are Thespian Shades for departed actors and Mr. Gillette could see what happened to the "efficient mechanical principles" of his locomotives, he would have had much cause for complaint to his executors!

Mount Gretna Narrow Gauge

Only one 2-foot-gauge railroad in American history ever possessed American type 4-4-0 locomotives and that was the Mount Gretna Narrow Gauge in Pennsylvania. The little line was essentially a project

Above are two scenes depicting the kind of motive power operated upon the one-mile railroad loop of the House of David at Benton Harbor, Mich. All were built by members of the sect. These have now all been sold and are supplanted by two modern Prairie (2-6-2) type locomotives, also built in the colony's shops.

for a recreational area, an amusement park on a grander scale, and was not precisely a common carrier as were its sister two-footers in the Maine woods. The Mount Gretna was, in fact, an offshoot of the standard-gauge Cornwall and Lebanon Railroad which opened a picnic ground at Mount Gretna, Lebanon County. The opening of the ground was almost immediaely followed by the designation of the territory west of Mount Gretna as a military reservation for the summer camps of the Pennsylvania National Guard. With Lake Conewago and the impressive peak of Governor Dick, it became a paradise for hikers; and early in the spring of 1889 Robert H. Coleman, who controlled the Cornwall and Lebanon, authorized the survey and construction of the road.

When built, the road was approximately four miles long from Mount Gretna to Governor Dick, with a branch to the National Guard Rifle Range. The motive power of the little road was quite outstanding. Two locomotives were ordered, one from the H. K. Porter Company and one from the Baldwin Locomotive Works. The Porter engine was an 0-4-4 Forney type hallowed by George Mansfield, the builder of the "two-foot empire" (See Chapter IV). The Baldwin engine, a 4-4-0, carried the road number 12 and was a miniature version of the Cornwall and Lebanon engines, even to the bright green paintwork and gleaming red driving wheels. The Forney's wheel base was too rigid for the sharp curves of the Mount Gretna line and it was retired. Baldwin turned out triplets in the 4-4-0 type locomotives; and the little system, after a busy five years of operation, went down in history as having owned and operated the only 2-foot-gauge, American type, live steamers in the United States.

Although abandoned as a recreational railroad, the Mount Gretna did operate to the Rifle Range (see map) at the behest of the Pennsylvania National Guard until 1915 when a curious accident finally gave it the quietus. A large number of guardsmen had climbed on to the footboard of the little cars which overturned on a sharp curve and resulted in some serious injuries. The line never recovered from an undeserved stigma. It was abandoned by all traffic from that time.

But long will the vacationers remember the Mount Gretna Railroad and the haul up the 2-foot-gauge track to the slopes of Governor Dick!

Sectarian Steamers

Remarkable among the 15-inch-gauge steam railroads in the United States is the one at Benton Harbor, Michigan. Built about 1908, the railroad is owned and operated by a religious sect known

Engine No. 4 has been dressed up in a form of streamlining hood and given a name as well. Individual observers will debate the artistry.

Engines No. 901, No. 902 and No. 903, which the House of David members built in 1948. Drivers are 16″ diameter; Cylinders 4″ x 5½″; wheelbase 8′-0″; height to top of stack 42″; length, engine and tender, 18′-0″; fuel anthracite coal; weight of engine 6,100 lbs.; tender 1,400 lbs.; tractive effort is 956 lbs.; steam pressure, 200 lbs.

as the House of David. Motive power, rolling stock and track were built by members who number approximately 1700 men, women and children and who live a self-supporting existence on a 1000-acre site of parkland, farm and orchard.

The founder of the group, Benjamin Franklin Purnell, was a somewhat controversial figure whose reputation as the Seventh Messenger and younger brother of Christ was marred by lawsuits and evidence that he led a double life in his Shiloh Palace as both Messenger and Caliph with several "wives." The elders who renounced him and took over the little colony perhaps lacked their old leader's brilliance and organizing abilities, but they at least cleaned house and insured the continuing success of this cooperative endeavor.

There were originally eight steam locomotives rebuilt in the House of David Shops. There were four 4-4-0's and four 4-6-0's, the latter having all main rods connected to the leading pair of drivers. Such practice is, of course, rare in full-scale locomotives. The 4-4-0's, quite obviously originally of Cagney manufacture, weighed 1800 pounds each and the 4-6-0's weighed 2200 pounds. All burned coal for fuel and operated under a head of 150 pounds of steam pressure. Standard equipment on the little engines were air brakes and two headlights.

The old locomotives were sold. They turn up every once in a while, one having been acquired by the W.F. & P. It was altered somewhat for use on that line. Still another was purchased from an intermediate owner by Mr. A. B. Jefferis of Piedmont, Missouri. He in turn resold it after operating it for one season. Some characteristics of the boilers of the House of David's old locomotives closely resemble Cagney types, but it is apparent these were of local manufacture.

The original stud was replaced in 1948 by three handsome Prairie 2-6-2's which weigh 7500 pounds each. The main line is in the form of an irregular loop a mile in circumference. All curves are banked, equipped with guard rails and are laid on oak ties. Trains are made up of eight passenger cars each seating eight people; and visitors in the vacation season make this attraction a profitable operation. The railroad is also a utility, for it hauls the men to work and brings back agricultural produce from the farm.

Unmarried men in this unusual sect wear their hair long. When they marry, they trim their hair and grow a beard. Ben Purnell preached that his true adherents were indestructible. Dogma is one thing, but it is quite certain that riding the sect's little railway is, for young and old alike, one of the most indestructible joys there is.

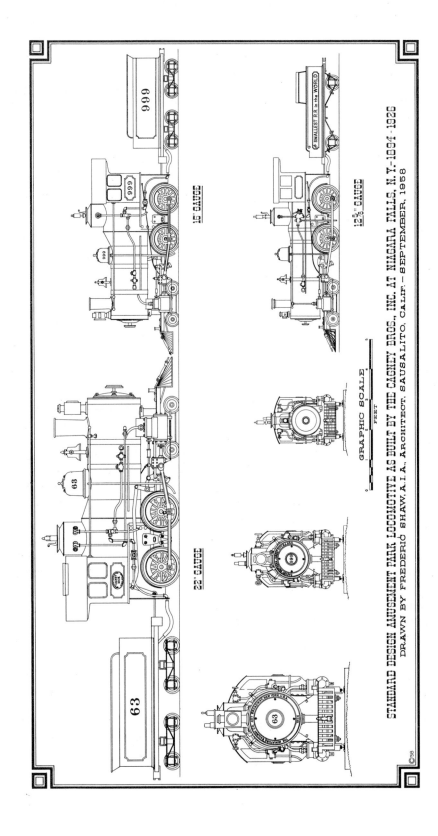

STANDARD DESIGN AMUSEMENT PARK LOCOMOTIVE AS BUILT BY THE CAGNEY BROS., INC. AT NIAGARA FALLS, N.Y.-1894-1926
DRAWN BY FREDERIC SHAW, A.I.A., ARCHITECT, SAUSALITO, CALIF.-SEPTEMBER, 1958

CHAPTER XV

THE BROTHERS CAGNEY

In the development of the park-size railway in the United States, no individuals have played a more important role than the brothers Cagney. Their contribution to the small-scale live steamer is a brand name which even today outshines those of many competitors. Possibly better locomotives have been built during the last half-century, but none have had such a durable quality as the chubby little Cagneys.

The Cagney brothers were not builders of miniature railways and never did actually fabricate an engine. They were promoters and brokers. And they were among the very first businessmen to recognize the need of the nation's amusement parks for more and better recreational facilities, particularly train rides. Mirrored in the Cagney locomotives of today one can see those loquacious Irishmen who had one foot in the antics of the *fin de siècle* and the other firmly planted in the 20th Century's Age of Steam. They had no monopoly in the market place, but in the words of the logistician, they got there "fastest with the mostest." As a matter of fact, over three thousand locomotives in the narrow gauges were fabricated for the Cagneys over the years.

Research has revealed the brothers were Timothy G. (President), David H. (Secretary-Treasurer), Charles L. and Thomas G. Records are silent as to what part Charles and Thomas played in the miniature train business. Their story probably has its beginning in an important event in the railroad history of the late Victorian era. This event was the breaking of the world speed record by the old New York Central and Hudson River Railroad's locomotive No. 999. The Cagneys took this prototype, whose great driving wheels are a reminder that speed is one of the biggest factors in the transportation business, and created a miniature live steamer to a one-sixth scale. The record run of the famed No. 999 between Syracuse and Buffalo, New York, on May 10, 1893, captured the public imagination. As the enterprising Cagneys had foreseen, young and old alike were fascinated by the thought of riding behind a smaller version of this greyhound of the rails.

The first locomotives built for the Cagneys were, by all good miniature standards, the best looking. They emerged around 1894 with

187

This Cagney 15″ gauge steam locomotive was owned by the House of David railroad where a new, deeper firebox was added, giving it the rather incongruous "too high" look.

A Cagney locomotive in 22-inch gauge in Lakeside Park, Denver, Colo. This engine is in "mint" condition, the photo apparently having been made shortly after arrival from the Cagney shops.

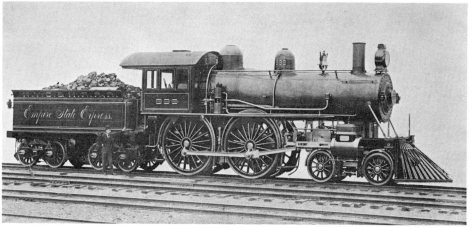

Famed engine No. 999 of the old New York Central & Hudson River R. R., built in 1893 by that railroad to haul its Empire State Express. It was the inspiration for the Cagney Brothers in their small locomotive building project which began in 1899 in Niagara Falls, N. Y.

The engine pictured here is what might be termed the only one still in possession of the Cagney family, for it belongs to Mr. Robert Parr who worked for Tim and David Cagney and has followed the amusement park business more or less since. The engine now operates under steam and its owner has added springs to the tender trucks. The headlight, marker lamps, steamchest end plate and crank on the main driving pin are all Parr additions to the original.

No. 999 blazoned on the cab. The one feature missing, characteristically a detail of their larger prototype, was the wagon-top at the rear of the boiler. Other details and proportions were in good scale, even to the long pointed pilot or "cowcatcher" and the cap stack. Some were built for a 12⅞-inch gauge and some for a 15-inch gauge, and all operated well on a level track. It soon became apparent, however, that more power was needed from a better steam generator, for they made heavy work with a paying load on even the slightest grade. A boiler larger in diameter was devised, still without the wagon top, with satisfactory results. Although the general design of the locomotive suffered, this larger boiler and small driving wheels increased the tractive effort and made it more efficient on normal, amusement park grades. A gesture was made toward the wagon-top boiler by resorting to a false "raise."

These first locomotives were equipped with 4-wheel tenders, sans springs. They were rough-riding vehicles for the engineer, a condition little mitigated by the advent of the double-truck tender, for it had no springs either. Another detail of manufacture adopted at the very outset of the firm's activities, was the sheet-steel boiler jacket. Generally, it was the practice to run this jacket from the inner end of the smokebox to the cab, but the Cagneys covered the whole length of the boiler, smokebox and all. This added materially to the finished appearance of the engine, as well as simplifying fabrication of the boiler inasmuch as the barrel was a single sheet of steel of the same diameter from front to firebox.

Early catalogs of the Cagneys noted that "one 0 Korting injector and one special pump" were supplied with each engine. Yet all their catalog illustrations showed an injector on each side of the engine. What the "special pump" was is not now known but presumably it was a force-feed pump operated from an eccentric on one of the driving axles.

The success of the larger boiler encouraged the Cagneys to turn out miniatures of 18-inch and 22-inch track gauge. These were uniformly built with wagon-top boilers. The 12⅞-inch gauge and 18-inch gauge miniatures were never popular; and it was not long before the brothers settled down "in the groove" and produced only the 15-inch and 22-inch gauge steam locomotives. Their advertising offered to make any gauge and type of steam locomotive "from 12⅞-inch gauge to standard gauge," an ambitious offer, but no record exists of any large-scale engine being built for them.

Several details of Cagney locomotive manufacture remained unchanged over the years. The steam dome casings of all early engines were fashioned of sheet metal. Somewhat later, however, both the sand dome and the steam dome were of cast iron, the profiles very closely following the simple but graceful design of late Baldwin locomotive manufacture. Many of both types are still extant on venerable Cagneys.

Early Cagney locomotives had one novel if "unorthodox" feature which lasted less than eight years of production; it was use of the handrails as lubricating lines from cab to steam chests. While novel and interesting, these lines, lacking any support to the boiler, were subject to injury and, if broken, would effectively cut off lubricant to the cylinders. Around the turn of the century this practice was dropped and the line was run from the cab, under the jacket and emerging therefrom at the smokebox to be attached to the top of the steam chest. This arrangement was never thereafter altered.

The oval nameplate appears to have been an adjunct not adopted until the very last years of the Cagneys' operations. A very few of their 4-4-0 locomotives of the last manufacture carried this metal emblem on their cab sides. It was applied to the very few Pacifics they made but was also uniform on all their gasoline-propelled versions of the simulated steam locomotives. Many of these are still extant.

Considering the length of time the Cagneys' business was so successful, it is remarkable that the basic design underwent so little change. The most conspicuous feature dropped was the long-pointed pilot. It had been built in two forms originally—a casting and also a fabricated type of round steel stock. Both were dropped in favor of a much shorter, stubby pilot of cast iron. The interesting push bar was eliminated too. Coincident with the change of pilot, the ornamental cap stack was dropped and a slightly tapered, beaded, cast stack substituted. This stack remained a standard for the rest of the manufacturing era.

The two injectors were uniformly supplied with each locomotive, the earliest being a "Century," a brand now long obsolete. Present-day Cagneys seem universally equipped with ⅜-inch Penberthy injectors. Brakes on engines were seldom supplied, nor were tender trucks ever equipped with springs. Some owners later supplied spiral springs. Steam brakes for locomotive drivers were, in the later years, supplied when ordered.

The very first versions of the Cagney steam locomotive emerged with headlights far removed from conventional design. They were

Herschell-Spillman Co. built this 15-gauge steam locomotive around the turn of the century. The train operated in Washington Park, Michigan City, Indiana.

If nothing else dated this photo, the attire of the amusement park's visitors surely would. A brand new Cagney locomotive specially attired in a gleaming, brass jacket and domes operating over the rails in Steeplechase Park at Coney Island, New York, in 1905.

An early version of a Cagney locomotive. The design was materially altered and improved over the early years until it was stereotyped and so remained until the end of the manufacturing era.

This 1910 photo of a 15-inch gauge original Cagney locomotive, was taken in Monarch Park, a 60-acre area about mid-way between Oil City and Franklin, Pennsylvania. A 5-cent fare gave a passenger a ride around 1,440 feet of the looped track. The park was owned by the Citizens Traction Company of Oil City. The original of this photo was exposed on a glass plate negative. The headlight is not a Cagney original and the smokestack has an appendage of doubtful worth.

nothing more than the popular bicycle "carbide" lamp. It was a standard item of equipment on the better "bikes." Both the 12⅜-inch and the 15-inch-gauge live steamers—known as Class C and D respectively—used this type of headlight, suitably nickel-plated!

Something approaching a locomotive headlight soon replaced the bicycle lamp. It was a square unit with a round base and ventilating bonnet. Of course, some owners frequently added their own versions. Some were crude in the extreme, but occasionally a skillful operator of a park-size locomotive fashioned an orthodox-looking headlight. In the last years of the manufacture of the standard 4-4-0 design, headlights were completely discarded. They never served any practical purpose, as night-time operation was rare.

The heyday of the Cagney era was just after World War I. Replicas of No. 999 steamed over the park-size railways of the world. In the United States they were legion; in England a novelty; Latin Americans clambered eagerly aboard the small trains; Siam, Russia, Japan, New Zealand, South Africa—all witnessed the coming of this sturdy little symbol of speed and patronized the little railways in increasing numbers. For years, the sturdiness, simplicity and dependability of the little Cagneys could not be matched.

But times change, even though the replicas of No. 999 did not. The early 1920's were restless times, and when employment slumped state legislators cast their eyes in every direction in an effort to create jobs. The National Association of Amusement Parks, Pools and Beaches had just adopted two feet as the official track gauge for park-size railways; and the operators themselves had fixed 90 pounds of steam pressure as the standard for miniature engines. The solons saw a single engineer piloting each train and felt there should be a fireman on board as well. Laws were enacted requiring the miniature steamer operating in a public area to carry both licensed engineer and fireman.

The results of this legislation were far-reaching and unexpected. Instead of creating thousands of new jobs, the law threatened the existence of a nation-wide industry. The tractive force of Cagney locomotives was high; but it did have its limits. They could not haul a two-man engine crew with a paying load of passengers. The problem posed for the park operators was simple: they had to use more powerful engines or scrap steam-operated railways.

From these days the heart seemed to go out of the Cagney enterprise. The brothers experimented with simulated steam locomotives powered with gasoline engines. The internal combustion engine was in many phases of industry—particularly in the automobile—coming

Author's Collection

This photo depicts what is probably a perfect version of a Cagney Brothers' standard design in 22-inch gauge. The headlight is not an original Cagney product.

Edw. T. Francis

One of the very few Cagney locomotives built to be propelled by a gasoline engine. This engine operates over the rails of the Black Diamond Miniature Railroad at Dover, New Jersey. A better designed cab would add materially to the locomotive's appearance.

Grandpa Rode Behind It

Need more be said? Part of a magazine advertisement of Cagney products, about 1900. The engine is an early version with the straight boiler, very soon discontinued.

Edw. T. Francis

The Cagney builder's plate attached to their later products. In the beginning of their venture, the name was cast along the periphery of the smokebox front and nearly all present day Cagneys still bear that identification.

into its own. The Cagneys designed many types and sizes of such units, and a Pacific engine did have a vogue for a while. A live steam Pacific also emerged and was given some acceptance by the park operators. But there were many rival models and the Cagney enterprise made little headway.

Four of the gas-engine type were sold to the miniature railway at Rye Beach, New York. They were not well designed, and although they conveyed passengers ashore over the long pier when steamers tied up, they served more as a utility than as a key attraction. Despite such concessions to the trend of the times, the Cagney fortunes declined by the mid-'Thirties to the point of extinction.

Human ambitions may be ephemeral things. But they sometimes leave a rich legacy. The Cagney's legacy is a host of live steamers still operating on the little railways of the world, evocative perhaps of a vanished era, yet reflecting a reawakening public interest in steam. The brothers remain, then as now, identified only as a brand name. Little is known of them as people. Where they were born and when they died is still missing from the record of the enterprise. A business address was first given as 301 Broadway, New York City; and in 1902 it was given as 407 Broadway in the same city. Apparently, removal of the business across the river to "Jersey" came some time later, for in 1926 they had an office and residence at 25 Nassau Place, East Orange, N.J. A city directory lists their last business address at 395 Ogden Avenue, Jersey City. According to Bob Parr, who in 1905 worked for the Cagneys at Mellville Park, Bayonne, New Jersey, they probably resided in Jersey City. Mr. Parr remembers that one of the Cagneys in his early years was a "ticket scalper" who bought and sold return stubs of railroad tickets. The rest is silence.

It was the maternal uncle, Peter H. McGarigle, who appears to have actually fabricated the Cagney locomotives and cars. He owned and operated the McGarigle Machine Company of Niagara Falls, New York. Born in the same city on December 21, 1863, Mr. McGarigle lived most of his adult life in the community. He had eight brothers and sisters. After being apprenticed to a machinist, he formed a partnership in 1892 with his brother Thomas. The machine shop was located on Second Street just off Main Street. It prospered from the beginning, concentrating right up into the 1920's in the booming demand for the Cagney live steamers. A newspaper of that time stated that McGarigle "has never been active in politics, but his opinions on all public questions are sound and sensible, embracing as they do considerations of the practical things of life."

The Cagney catalogues reminded potential customers that the little locomotives received gold medals at all expositions. The King of Siam ordered his Cagneys to be nickel-plated!

"Gold Medal Specials," as the Cagneys termed them, almost completed at Mc-Garigle Machine Company shop, Niagara Falls, New York. The little locomotives are 15-inch-gauge Class D versions with the standard carbide bicycle lamps!

The practical things of life were, without question, an engineering skill which, added to the business enterprise of the Cagneys, gave the world a remarkable little steam locomotive. From Siam to San Francisco, and from New Zealand to New York, the Cagney versions of the famed old No. 999 have puffed. They are still bought and sold, altered, modified, reboilered—yet remain recognizable to the Cagney student. A roster of existing locomotives would, with a thumbnail sketch of their checkered careers, provide a fascinating epitaph for the headstone of these loquacious Irishmen who, though vexing the railroad historian in search of the facts of their personal lives, have given more pleasure to the public than any other promoters of miniature railways.

MINIATURE RAILROAD COMPANY,

(INCORPORATED.)

Inventores, Fabricantes y Exportadores de Ferrocarriles ligeros completos.

Locomotora Ligera Para Ingenios y la Industria, Contratistas y todos los demás usos.

El Ferrocarril de Vapor más pequeño del mundo. Conduce 20 pasageros, y usa carbón como combustible. La mayor atracción y el mejor negocio para hacer dinero del siglo **XX**.

CAGNEY'S LOCOMOTIVE WORKS, Oficina 301 Broadway, New York, E. U. A.

CABLE: "MINRAILCO," CLAVE LIEBER.

From the earliest times the Cagney miniatures found a ready market in Latin America, as evidenced by this page from a Spanish language catalogue which the promotion-minded brothers circulated widely.

This hybrid Cagney 22-inch gauge locomotive hauls thousands of happy passengers at Fleishhacker Zoo and is a most profitable business venture for the city of San Francisco. The boiler is not of Cagney manufacture nor shape but was fashioned by city mechanics in the very early 1940's.

A low angle shot of *Cricket*. From this viewpoint it is sometimes hard to believe one is looking at a miniature live steamer whose diamond stack is less than shoulder height.

CHAPTER XVI

BAY AREA STEAM BANTAMS

The Fleishhacker Zoo Railroad, San Francisco
The Tilden, South Gate and Pacific Railroad, Berkeley
The Oakland Narrow Gauge Railroad

MUNICIPAL VENTURES INTO the realm of recreational attractions are not particularly noteworthy from the standpoint of yielding a profit. In fact, most of them operate in the red. This may be deemed a taxpayer contribution to the amenities of the city parks. And most of us make no complaint. But it is gratifying nonetheless when a recreational feature turns a neat little profit.

Such is the case with the miniature steam railway at Fleishhacker Zoo Park in San Francisco. And indications are that the other cities of the Bay Area appear to find the maintenance of miniature railroad systems profitable in terms of human happiness and are at least able to break even. Both Oakland and Berkeley have steam-hauled lines as well, but it would be hard to find three cities with such a variety of design in motive power, rolling stock and track layout.

The senior locomotive in point of age is a real little aristocrat of the 22-inch-gauge, a Cagney 4-4-0 operating at Fleishhacker Zoo. The "littlest fellah" is next in seniority and his name is *Cricket*. He is a chirpy 12-inch-gauge live steamer who operates in Tilden Regional Park. The biggest of the three and also the youngest is the *Oakland Acorn,* a fine looking Pacific operating on a 16-inch-gauge line in Peralta Playground in the city of Oakland. It is a worthy triumvirate to uphold the best traditions of park-size live steamers.

Thirty or forty years ago, Cagney steam locomotives were almost a commonplace in amusement parks all over the country. They were the sturdiest of the sturdy and ranked among the best for longevity. They were keenly bid for when up for sale, and they migrated far and wide. The San Francisco Park and Recreation Department was very fortunate in securing one in 1925 which, despite its several alterations and modifications, is recognizable to the Cagney student. It was put to work in those far-off days on a 1000 ft. loop just a few yards removed from Ocean Beach and the flaunting Pacific. Not too much imagination was used in the building of this loop, although it was rebuilt and lengthened in the Spring of 1948 to 1880 feet, a 60-foot trestle added

Cricket, an Ottaway-built 12-inch gauge locomotive as altered by its owner who made the diamond stack, headlight, wood cab and long pilot to approximate a diamond stacker of the 1890's. This little engine draws people from near and far, and operates in Tilden Park, Berkeley, California, atop the hills back of the city.

A Tilden South Gate & Pacific Freight in one of the cuts of this scenic little line approximately one mile in circumference.

A view of the recent landslide on the Tilden Park line. Below the broken rail is the half-buried caboose. Operator and municipal authorities moved in heavy equipment and the 12-inch gauge railway was restored to working order in less than two weeks.

Mud baths are reputedly of therapeutic worth. Not so this one. The trim little *Cricket* as it appeared after being dragged from the depths of the slide that all but wrecked it for good.

and the track re-ballasted and aligned on level ground at a cost of $18,720.

In 1936, the little Cagney was sent to the municipal machine shops and there reboilered, the original boiler being discarded. No attempt was made to copy the outlines of the wagon-top Cagney boiler. Instead, an extended wagon-top design was adopted, the slope starting at the smokebox and lifting to the position of the rear tube sheet. Not as attractive as the original, it is admittedly a better steam generator and serves the engine more efficiently. Unfortunately for the purists, the Russian iron jacket was not restored. A stainless steel covering was substituted.

To the vast majority of patrons, however, a ride is a ride when it comes to steam-hauled park trains; and if passenger receipts are any indication a 5-cent ticket on the little Zoo railway remains one of the city's best bargains.

Your chronicler on many a warm Sunday afternoon in the late 'Thirties used to relieve Peter Neilson, the engineer at the throttle of the gleaming Cagney, and having collected the tickets, piloted the train around the loop while Pete took a brief respite over his lunch bucket. He loved his job and came to know so many of his regular customers among the children. He retired on June 28, 1940, and was succeeded by an engineer born to the part.

Unlike Pete who was a stationary engineer originally, Howard "Casey" Jones was an engineer retired from piloting Class I railroad live steamers. He called off mythical station destinations such as "Askidopolis", "Ice Cream Soda Springs", "Snigglefritz", and while collecting tickets from the small fry went through an act of miming that a Hollywood comedian would envy. It was worth a long trip to stand at the Zoo station and watch while he pretended the engine would not budge when he opened the throttle. His miming continued as he sat on his tender perch and piloted the little train around the loop.

In one sense, the Zoo's little Cagney bears the imprint of Mac-Dermot of "Exposition Pike" fame. "Mac" furnished a new bell and bell-frame and a headlight when the engine was reboilered. The headlight is never illumined, but the bell gets a good workout each trip.

We re-cross the sparkling blue waters of San Francisco Bay to visit the Tilden, South Gate & Pacific Railway. In the wooded hills east of the city of Berkeley runs a quite spectacular double loop line of track. Motive power is the diamond-stack *Cricket*, a 12-inch-gauge steamer which instantly becomes the idol of every boy and girl who sets eyes upon it. Conceived and built over a period of two years by Erich Thomsen, a young mechanical engineer employed by the Western Pacific Railroad, motive·power and track layout are among the most outstanding in the West. Thomsen purchased the chassis and boiler from an established locomotive builder and set to work with his own hands and machine tools to create a Victorian-era diamond-stacker. It was a shoe-string operation from the start but dedication to the task has paid off handsomely and the attractions of *Cricket* are known and discussed far and wide.

The track laying operation was another formidable task for a busy mechanical engineer. The rail is 12-lb. flat bottomed on redwood ties with a few lengths, mostly in sidings, of 10-lb. rail. The route, which is well graded and ballasted, takes the visitor through several cuts, over fills and a well-built wood trestle.

Unseasonal rains in the San Francisco Bay Area in the Spring of 1958 brought disaster to the little line. On the afternoon of April 8, the rain-soaked area at the head of a steep gulch on which stood the engine house and store room started to slide. In less time than it takes to write these words, the slide had taken the engine house, including *Cricket* and equipment, and almost buried it. The only thing visible through the mud was the little diamond stack of the *Cricket*.

Municipal authorities lent a willing hand with machinery and equipment. A line was somehow secured beneath the engine's main frames and the engine hauled out of its mudbath. Subsequent examination revealed that the mud had completely filled smokebox and flues, lifted the grates clear up to the crownsheet, knocked off and buried the ornamental cover to the sand dome and twisted the woodwork so badly out of shape it was necessary to remove it. Further search in the mud brought out the engine truck and the tender (minus one truck which has not yet been recovered) and all the passenger cars. Such is Thomsen's energy and spirit that, despite a rerouting of the track, rehabilitation of the little railway occupied only two weeks. A new engine terminal and yards are projected to supplant the ones destroyed.

Trains on the Tilden, South Gate & Pacific Railway operate only on Saturdays and Sundays. According to Erich Thomsen, the line presently just about breaks even from the financial standpoint despite its great popularity. He has been turning over in his mind plans for an even more scenic line with fifteen-inch-gauge motive power and rolling stock. If this ever comes to pass, the whole Bay Area will mourn the little *Cricket*.

Our last call on the miniature railway systems of the Bay Area is at Peralta Playground in the city of Oakland. Still fresh in the mem-

Harold Winder

The 15-inch gauge *Oakland Acorn* standing at the main depot in Peralta Playground, Oakland. So well designed and built is this "Pacific" beauty that scarcely a cent has been expended on repairs since she was built in 1949.

Harry L. Dixon

Gene Autry, the famous cowboy actor, owns and operates this handsome 18-inch gauge steam streamliner *Melody Ranch Special,* to haul visitors around. George A. Reddington, seated at the controls, built this locomotive and cars as well as the *Oakland Acorn* 15-inch gauge for the City of Oakland, California. Both locomotives burn stove oil for fuel.

ory of most Californians are recollections of the handsome, colorful steam behemoths which hauled the Southern Pacific "Daylights" between San Francisco and Los Angeles. These great locomotives were the inspiration of model-maker and artist alike — and, be it added, of the builders of the park-size miniatures. The engine, ordered by Oakland's Park Department from George A. Reddington and Robert E. Blécha, departed in a small way from the main line prototype in that it is a Pacific type 4-6-2 and the "Daylight" goliaths were Mountain type 4-8-4's. But the builders, both tool and die makers, did a magnificent job and produced a small locomotive as perfect as could be fashioned by human hands. The greatest testimony one could pay makers and operators alike resides in the fact that scarcely a cent has been spent on maintenance in the whole ten years of its existence.

Since the train went into operation, an automatic counter at the last switch prior to entering the terminal has registered a total of over 13,000 miles. It is quite an achievement for a miniature train traveling a loop of less than one-half mile. But that one-half mile is packed with interest. Leaving the depot, the train starts toward the Oakland estuary, crosses the salt tidal stream in a tunnel which serves as night housing for the train, turns to the left upstream toward East 14th Street, then again crosses the estuary, which here is underground, and returns to the playground area, making another small loop through a series of switches to resume the main line and the terminal.

Painted in the rich orange and red of the famed "Daylights" the passenger cars resemble their big sisters. Visitors enter them on the right side the other side being painted to resemble car windows. The moving train creates a fine illusion of looking at the big prototypes.

The locomotive, named the *Oakland Acorn,* burns stove oil for fuel and raises an operating head of 150 lbs. of steam. It is equipped with air pump and air brakes, as are all the passenger cars. One remarkable fact about the passenger equipment is that every wheel runs on ball or roller bearings and can be easily pushed by hand. *Oakland Acorn,* which was built for a 16-inch-gauge, weighs 4000 lbs. in operating order.

Gene Autry, the noted cowboy actor, was so impressed with the *Oakland Acorn* that he ordered a replica for his ranch in Southern California. It was delivered early in 1958. Autry plans a 3-mile railway for operation next year; and we have mentally made reservations for a conducted tour and a place for a story in further chronicles of miniature railways.

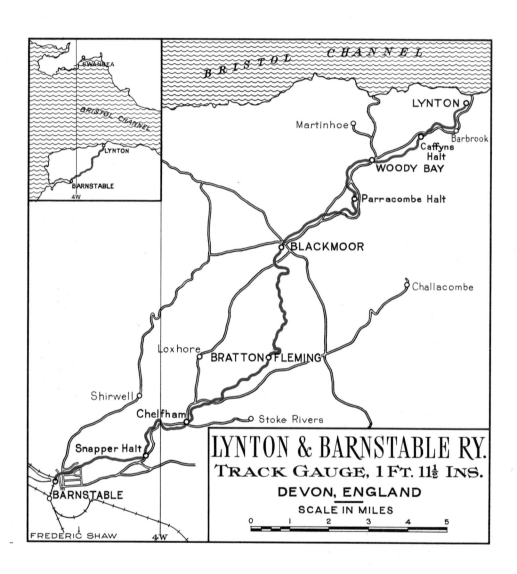

BRISTOL CHANNEL

SWANSEA

BRISTOL CHANNEL

LYNTON

BARNSTABLE

4W

LYNTON

Martinhoe

Barbrook

Caffyns
Halt

WOODY BAY

Parracombe Halt

BLACKMOOR

Challacombe

Loxhore

BRATTON FLEMING

Shirwell

Chelfham

Stoke Rivers

Snapper Halt

BARNSTABLE

FREDERIC SHAW   4W

LYNTON & BARNSTABLE RY.
TRACK GAUGE, 1 FT. 11½ INS.
DEVON, ENGLAND
SCALE IN MILES

0   1   2   3   4   5

CHAPTER XVII

SURVIVAL OF THE FITTEST

The Lynton and Barnstable Railway
The Vale of Rheidol Railway

IN BRITAIN THEY sometimes call them "toy" railways. They are the two footers which are somehow surviving the twilight of the narrow gauge. It is not good to call them toy, for that suggests playthings. Yet railroaders take them seriously. Had they been taken seriously at all times they would not have expired, like the Lynton and Barnstable Railway in North Devon, which was strangely ill-starred from the beginning.

There are two narrow gauge lines in Britain's history, built within six years of one another, operated in their later years with all the resources of Class I railways, yet one survives and the other is gone. One line has weathered changing times and economic storms; the other seemed to fumble its way along, yielding to every adverse circumstance because men were not serious enough about her.

The line that survives is the Vale of Rheidol Railway; the one that expired amid thoughtless fanfares of farewell was the lovely Lynton line. This chapter will attempt to trace their checkered careers and weigh some of the facts that balanced the scales between life and death.

The Lynton and Barnstable Railway traversed the wild and beautiful upland country known as Exmoor, immortalized in Blackmore's *Lorna Doone*. Combes or valleys thread the rolling, heather-covered hills, not only unfavorable in their direction for a line from Barnstable to Lynton but also excessively steep at the head end. It seems that the Lynton residents pressed hardest for a connecting link between Barnstable, on the banks of the River Yeo, and the lovely twin villages of Lynton and Lynmouth on the North Devon coast; and when the standard gauge roads declined to take an interest, the promoters cited the example of the narrow gauges of Wales. In fact the original prospectus stated that "as many as thirty-four horse coaches and brakes (stage coaches) enter Lynton every day in the season. . . . This traffic", the prospectus added, "will be increased by the pleasure of traveling on a line of the same nature as the famous Festiniog. . . ."

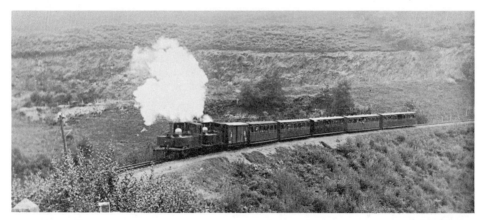

R. W. Kidner

Double header on the Lynton and Barnstable's 19 miles of railroading delight. The line was somewhat ill-starred from the beginning; but one can only exclaim as Shakespeare: "The fault, dear Brutus, lies in ourselves, not in our stars." It was human error that brought the line to a close.

The Times, London—"London Daily Express"

Barnstable to Lynton train, headed by Manning, Wardle locomotive 2-6-2T No. 761 near Lynton. A wreath was laid on the line when it closed in 1935 with the inscription: "Perchance she is not dead, but sleepeth." The little railway certainly lives on in the minds of all who traveled those Exmoor valleys in the swaying 2-foot-gauge cars which thudded at the rail joints as the train entered places of blessed memory like Blackmoor Gate, Chelfham, Woody Bay and the rather inaccessible Lynton itself.

The Lynton and Barnstable Railway Bill received the Royal Assent on June 27, 1895; it authorized a capital of 70,000 pounds. The first sod was turned on September 17, 1895, amid great celebrations. However, actual construction did not get under way until March, 1896. The surveyed line was "19 miles, 1 furlong and 5 chains long", starting at a joint station in Barnstable with the old London and Southwestern Railway and ending somewhat shyly at the top of a hill "so that it will not be visible from Lynton and Lynmouth". Nobody can deny that the desired invisibility was achieved, although at the price of accessibility.

The survey proved unfortunate in more ways than the location of the northern terminal. Throughout the whole of Exmoor, outcroppings of red Devon rock are visible, but apparently little consideration was given to this factor. The contractor, who soon went bankrupt, anticipated nothing more than earth-moving problems. The estimated costs were 2,500 pounds per mile and the actual cost when completed, due to the continuous blasting necessary, was in excess of 5,000 pounds per mile. The price of land and compensation for the right-of-way turned out to be four times the estimated figure. Annual income was estimated at 12,000 pounds, but only half that sum was realized. Complaints about the rocking of the cars added to the troubles of the little railway. There were also complaints about the speed of the trains which were of "mixed consist" and took a hundred minutes to cover the nineteen miles and shunt freight at the various stations.

Motive power, however, was not responsible for slothful performance. The equipment was in fact far above the average for the type of line. The three 2-6-2T locomotives constructed by Manning, Wardle & Co. of Leeds and the 2-6-2T Baldwin with bar frames were all excellent performers; but the track, though good, lacked the solidity of Spooner's Festiniog and the sharper curves of the Lynton line were not easily traversed by the six-coupled steamers. The rolling of engine and cars was not just fancy on the part of passengers.

Sir George Newnes, the noted British publisher and the chief promoter of the line, realized the publicity value of well kept stations and awarded an annual prize for the best floral display. Flowers beside the track were fostered by the Rev. J. F. Chanter whose habit it was to broadcast seed from the car windows. But it was profits not posies the Lynton line needed and this rather placid existence ended in March 1923 when it was purchased by the Southern Railway. This Class I railroad immediately carried out a number of improvements, including complete reballasting of track and new ties. Train working was

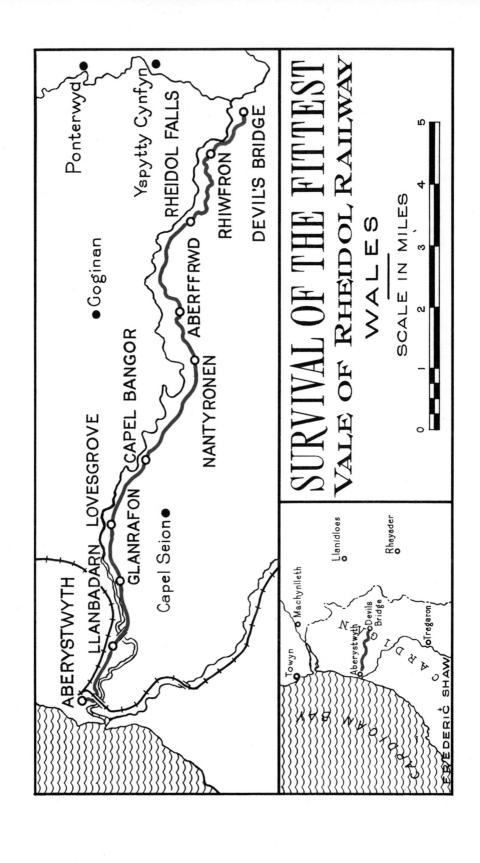

SURVIVAL OF THE FITTEST
VALE OF RHEIDOL RAILWAY

WALES

SCALE IN MILES

FREDERIC SHAW

improved, the right-of-way fenced and station accommodation enlarged. Rolling stock was overhauled and seats upholstered. All these improvements were insufficient to secure the line from the steadily increasing competition of the automobile and local support almost completely vanished. The days of the Lynton & Barnstable were numbered.

During the months that elapsed between the first announcement of proposed abandonment and actual sale, there was some effort to stay the hand of Fate. But when a protest meeting was held at Barnstable, all the delegates from Lynton arrived *by automobile!* The sale of the railroad was accomplished on Wednesday, November 13, 1935. Only three hundred people had turned up the previous September to take their long farewell. One locomotive survived the junk yard. *Lew,* one of the 2-6-2T Manning Wardle engines, returned to its maker for overhaul and final shipment to a coffee plantation in Brazil. The earthworks remain, and the great viaduct at Chelfham which spanned the Stokes River valley, but they are earthworks that might have been left by the ancient Romans. The Lynton and Barnstable Railway has gone.

The Vale of Rheidol Railway got its fair share of complaints too. In the early days passengers sometimes complained, according to an excellent booklet compiled by Lewis Cozens, that they would never again risk their lives in a train which traversed such an awe-inspiring track. And a highly placed official from one of the leading British railroads who had a wooden leg, had his nerves so badly frayed that he vowed he would walk back to the seaport terminal rather than return by train. Both the Lynton and the Rheidol sold views of great beauty for the price of a ticket, but there was a world of difference between a nineteen mile stretch connecting two sleepy Devon towns and a twelve mile ride up a mineral-rich valley far closer to dense population centers of Britain's industrial Midlands. Coal, copper ore, lead, timber — all lay in the Vale of Rheidol and were good and sufficient reasons why on August 6, 1897, the company was incorporated with the object of building a narrow gauge railway from Aberystwyth, a progressive resort on the Cardiganshire coast of Wales, and Devil's Bridge. The line was capitalized at £39,000 and was not completed, according to the contract for £51,000, until the summer of 1902; but the cost per mile, on an alignment calling for just as skillful engineering, compared very favorably with the Lynton and Barnstable Railway.

The Vale of Rheidol Railway, built to the 60 centimeter gauge (23.62 inches), was popular from the beginning. And one can see why when reading articles by Mr. James Rees in the *Welsh Gazette:*

Paul Popper Ltd.

At the sheds in Aberystwyth, the coastal resort terminal of the Vale of Rheidol Railway. British Railways, which operate the line, open it for only three summer months; but so great a tourist attraction is it that tens of thousands of vacationers flock there each year, and, at 2 shillings and nine pence (38 cents) for the round trip, a very healthy revenue is garnered.

Paul Popper Ltd.

Leaving Aberffrwd on the Vale of Rheidol Railway's slim-gauge pike to Devil's Bridge. With mountains on one side of the track and sheer precipices on the other, it is not hard to imagine the fears of passengers in the early days of operation. Devil's Bridge got its name from a legend about an old woman who wanted to cross the ravine. The Devil's price for the bridge was the soul of the first living creature to cross—which happened to be a dog.

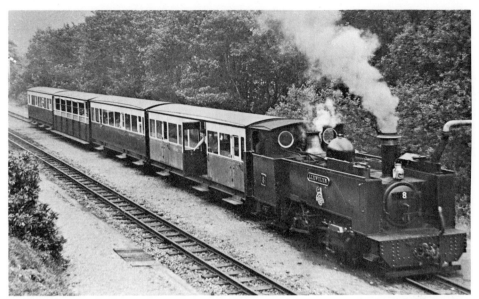

Paul Popper Ltd.

No. 8 *Llywelyn*, a 2-6-2T engine built at the Swindon shops of British Railways in 1923, is watered at Aberffrwd. The engine requires another 300 gallons of water for the final haul to Devil's Bridge. Grades from this point are almost constantly 2 per cent on the lovely, legend-haunted little railway.

Paul Popper Ltd.

Akin to some humans, locomotives develop tremendous thirsts. No. 8 has stopped at a water crane to slake her thirst then hustle on down the main over the almost miniature two-foot-gauge rails.

"The cost of handling coal and lime from Aberystwyth to Devil's Bridge and ore in the opposite direction was fixed at 2s. 3d. (54c) a ton, which was less than one-fifth of the charge by road. The cost of transshipping mineral traffic such as coal and lime from standard gauge to narrow gauge and ore in the reverse direction was 3d. (6c) per ton. Farmers ordered lime and fertilizers extensively and householders around Devil's Bridge were able to get their coal supplied at less cost than the ruling price in Aberystwyth. The supply of foodstuffs became more abundant and less costly. A much needed fillip was given to the lead mining industry in the district: more money was spent on development schemes and more men found profitable employment. In fact the new railway brought about a most gratifying increase in the prosperity of the people of the surrounding district. . . ."

The passenger trains were well patronized, especially on market and fair days, but the greatest benefit which the railway brought in this direction was the development of the tourist industry. The little Rheidol took visitors up this, one of the loveliest of Welsh valleys, at less than half the cost of stage coach. The line was always well publicized, for the first general manager, James Rees, traveled abroad and brought back from Switzerland ideas for some striking posters which were displayed as far away as Birmingham and London.

In 1909 timber trucks were skillfully adapted with ornamental metal and reversible seats for open passenger cars; and so successful was this venture that an extra charge of 3d (6c) had to be made. Nothing like this was tried on the Lynton railway.

In 1912 came the end of a very busy spell at the Rheidol Mine. In the same year a prominent electric traction company approached the Rheidol with a view to acquiring all interests and converting it into an electric tramway. While negotiations were proceeding the standard gauge Cambrian Railway took over controlling interest, thus ending an era of great enterprise and prosperity.

The war years 1914-18 were marked by fitful activity in the mines and greatly reduced passenger services. The Great Western Railway absorbed the Cambrian in 1923 and thus the little Rheidol changed hands a second time. However, this new ownership was more enterprising and all motive power and rolling stock was overhauled. The narrow gauge was extended from its old depot to a common terminal with the main line. Despite improvements in service winter passenger traffic ceased in 1931. But apart from the years of the Second World War when the line was closed, the Rheidol has been maintained at a high operating efficiency. This "cared for" appearance has lasted to the present day. The best footnote to the little railway is contributed by James Rees, its first manager, writing in the *Welsh Gazette* in April, 1949:

"As long as the gross earnings from the traffic bear a favorable relation to the expenditure, the future of the railway may be secure, but if it does not pay its way it may suffer the fate of other small railways. When the railway was independent the heavy passenger traffic which it carried was largely attracted by extensive advertising, by pictorial posters and other devices but since its transfer to the larger corporations scarcely anything has been done to bring its charms to the notice of visitors. It is a remarkable tribute to its popularity, however, that notwithstanding this handicap, enormous crowds continue to patronize it during the summer months."

Mr. Rees goes on to say that "its construction involved a vast amount of labor, energy and money, which was provided entirely by private enterprise . . ." It is the private enterprise element in railroading that revived the Festiniog. It was lacking in the Lynton line when local people failed to give it serious support and go all out to attract the lucrative tourist trade. For there is a strong feeling abroad in Britain that the little live steamers and the fun and joy of riding in the cars they haul has a place even in the most modern economy. This mental climate did not exist in 1935. Even the people who control the Government operated British Railways are aware of this trend and, possibly needled by Mr. Rees, are publicizing widely one of their proudest possessions. Connecting main line travel is being provided. And if passengers complain about the hair-raising precipices the narrow gauge line skirts, so much the better. It will make other people want to travel over the Vale of Rheidol all the more.

B. W. Koob

Engine No. 2967 crossing the shorter, 70-foot trestle over the creek with the entire passenger stock on a week-end day. Trips over the line on operating days generally terminated at 9:00 p.m.

C. T. Steeb

What the passenger consist looked like when first built by the Burlington R.R. for advertising purposes in street parades. Bought by the Hiatt interests the bodies were denuded of their road wheels and 4-wheel trucks fitted to them for the two-foot track gauge.

CHAPTER XVIII

FOOTPLATES AND FANCIES

The Byron Railroad—
The Wildcat Railroad—
The Far Tottering and Oyster Creek Railway—
The Lancaster and Chester Park Railroad

FROM THE CAB footplate of the miniature steam locomotive the world is full of fancy! The low elevation, the narrow gauge track, the little bridges and stations afford the illusion of a journey back in time to a favorite haunt which has unaccountably become smaller than it was when we first remembered it. How things shrink—the old swimming hole on the boyhood stream, the elm-shaded street, the bedroom below which the cock crowed! The pang that comes with seeing again these old haunts is nothing but a sense of loss. We have outgrown something infinitely precious.

The engineer in the cab of his miniature live steamer is in a different position. He is taking a similar journey back in time, but the meandering railroad he finds himself in is a world of his own creation. It is such a complete system along his right-of-way that even the big farm horse looking over the fence and kicking up his heels is an interloper and something of a sceptic. The two-tone station wagon that unloads its passengers at the miniature terminal for a train ride belongs to the crowded freeways and a life the engineer has long since abandoned. The little live steamer is not concerned with arriving at a destination but in puffing along a steam trail infinitely superior to macadam. And steam trails, like Indian trails, do not in their very nature lead anywhere. They are worlds of fancy and should be treated as such.

The engineer who creates little railways is naturally concerned with fashioning locomotives, cars and stations and with laying track. In that sense he is a practical man. But beyond this, he is creating only the physical framework of a world in miniature in which those who board its trains accept the fancies of the cab footplate.

The Byron Railroad

Twenty years ago at Creston, Iowa, a plumber and steam fitter started to create the physical framework of a miniature railway sys-

To give even wear to the wheels of the road's equipment, train travel is periodically reversed. Here engine No. 2968 is on the short trestle going in the reversed direction.

A double-header coming down off Mocking Bird Hill with a passenger drag behind. A pure publicity stunt, this superfluous power show was put on for the public on popular holidays—July Fourth, Labor Day, etc. The telegraph lines in the background are scaled down to the proportions of the two-foot-gauge line.

No. 2967 crossing the 80-foot steel trestle on the old (Creston) site dragging the road's passenger consist behind as smoke from the locomotive's stack trails off in the breeze.

A rather nostalgic shot of the passenger consist crossing the long trestle as the train moves into the cut on an upgrade to the top of Mocking Bird Hill. "MARY ETTA LIMITED" is on the rear of the observation car.

Harry Dixon

Another 18″ gauge locomotive designed by John Cort for the Venice Ry. which was retrieved from a Los Angeles junk yard and rebuilt by Wm. Jones of Los Gatos, California, for operation on his ½-mile orchard loop. Mr. Jones reinstalled the 2-wheel trailing truck since photo was made.

Author's Collection

The city of Venice, California, is on the ocean beach near Los Angeles. In the early days of its development the only available transportation was the 18-inch-gauge steam lines traversing the streets and the numerous canal bridges. Above is engine No. 2 of the Venice Railway. This engine now operates at Los Gatos, California, every week-end.

tem. Today, not many miles away at Martinsdale, Iowa, the little railway is completed, fashioned in the main by his own hands.

The plumber and steam fitter was Byron Hiatt. At one time he worked on a railroad, but a physical impairment disqualified him from road service. When one day he found at the Davenport Locomotive Works in Davenport, Iowa, two 2-foot-gauge chassis he decided to build his own road. He quickly turned up the first boiler. It belonged to an old threshing machine. The second boiler Mr. Hiatt needed was discovered at a nearby creamery. Adapting the two steam generators to his two chassis was not an easy task. The operation took many months of trial and error. But eventually there emerged from the Hiatt "shops" near Creston two locomotives which looked as if they had been fabricated by a professional builder.

The track was laid after Mr. Hiatt had completed a tour of duty with the Army in World War II. For rolling stock he located a baggage car and day coach fashioned for advertising purposes in street parades. The Byron Railroad, as it was called, was opened for business in the summer of 1950. So successful was that first year of operation that two thousand people were carried, on trains operating only at weekends, at 25 cents a head.

Since 1950, business has increased to the point where Mr. Hiatt has had to abandon Creston and relocate his road on a larger site at Martinsdale. A longer and more varied ride is provided on 35 lb. and 50 lb. rail spiked to discarded Burlington ties. The track is well ballasted with crushed rock. In fact, every detail along the right-of-way is perfect.

For design and efficiency the two Byron Railroad locomotives would be hard to beat. Purists may criticise the placing of the smokestack of No. 2967 forward of the cylinders, but there are undoubtedly good mechanical reasons for this. No. 2967 has been given the name of *Byron* and No. 2968 is named *Manfred* in honor of Manfred Hiatt, the engineer's brother. The numbers belonged to Burlington locomotives the brothers much admired. The passenger train honors the name of Mr. Hiatt's mother. Her name, *Mary Etta,* appears on the rear of the observation car.

Who but a miniature railroad engineer, gazing from the cab of his live steamer, can create such an ageless world?

Wildcat Railroad

Another engineer who goes his journeys back in time aboard his own live steamer is Billy Jones of Los Gatos, California. Mr. Jones befriended Louis MacDermot of "Exposition Pike" fame (see Chapter II) in the latter's last illness. It was probably a mutual resolve on the part of the two men that the Overfair Railway equipment should augment train operations on Billy Jones' "Wildcat Railroad." The Exposition Pacifics, the 0-6-0T switcher, rolling stock and many extra parts were trucked to the Jones ranch home at Los Gatos and stored.

MacDermot's switcher was completely restored and the 1900-foot loop of track widened from the existing 18-inch-gauge to 19-inch-gauge. But the curves of the loop proved too sharp for the little Exposition switcher and the track was again altered back to its original gauge of 18 inches.

The Wildcat Railroad's own locomotive has an interesting history. Originally it was one of the 2-6-2 type, 18-inch-gauge live steamers which furnished the motive power for the only street car service in Venice, California. Two of them were shunted off the miniature railroad map into Southern California junkyards.

In the mid-'Thirties Billy Jones found one of them in a San Francisco junkyard and promptly bought it for $100.00. How it found its way up north without a tender is anybody's guess. Mr. Jones was at that time an active engineer aboard the famed Southern Pacific's "Daylight" and arranged to send the little live steamer to his Company's Mission Bay shops, San Francisco, where she was restored to full working order. Since there was no tender, a short, Vanderbilt-type tender was fashioned and the motive power unit painted in the glowing red and orange colors of the "Daylight."

Acquiring sufficient light rail, Mr. Jones laid out over his Los Gatos ranch a 1900-foot loop which skirted his prune orchards and included one rather sharp grade on a curve. The track is maintained in excellent condition, affording a smooth, pleasant ride in the 16-seat, open, canopied cars of the old Exposition. They have proved more adaptable than the switcher!

Not skilled in the use of machine tools, Mr. Jones attended night school and became proficient in fabricating the needed parts for repairs. His terminal facilities include a machine shop, a 14-foot turntable, a 4-stall engine shed for the Exposition's 19-inch-gauge equipment and one for the ex-Venice live steamer. These facilities include a summer arbor with picnic tables for the constant stream of visitors. The Wildcat Railroad is operated only at weekends and holidays but certain days are set aside for charitable organizations—mostly orphanages—when the children are given free rides and a big picnic spread afterwards in the arbor.

A notable addition to the Wildcat's motive power will be in service early in 1959. Mr. Jones purchased from John Knowles of Burton on Trent, England, a most unusual 18-inch-gauge live steamer. It is a 0-4-0T beauty built in 1951 by the Hunslett Engine Company of Leeds. She is named *Queen* and operates on a boiler pressure of 160 lbs., and it is certain she will have many admirers at Los Gatos.

This is Mr. Jones' world of fancy—a meandering miniature railroad world with no destination or goal but the delight of children. With that mischievous twinkle in his eye and singular warmth of welcome for young and old alike, he is an unforgettable personality; and it is not beyond the realm of possibility that he will one day find a way of enlarging his Wildcat Railroad for the operation of the Exposition Pike's Pacifics.

Far Tottering and Oyster Creek Railway

Although no engineer by background or training, the British artist, Rowland Emett, is full of the engineer's fancy. His "Far Tottering and Oyster Creek Railway" was created for cartoons and the pages of London's *Punch;* but the railway of our childhood dreams was given corporate existence at the Festival of Britain in 1952. It was built by S. and B. Miniature Railways, Ltd. to Emett's designs and proved to be one of the greatest attractions at Battersea Park, London, where the Festival was held. The single track, of 15-inch-gauge, ran for a third of a mile around the southern perimeter of the gardens, and had one short tunnel and two terminals. Oyster Creek terminal had a distinctly nautical flavor, reminiscent of a semi-derelict fisherman's hut. Far Tottering was equally eccentric but possessed a refreshment bar.

Of the three locomotives, No. 1 *Nellie* was the more orthodox from Emett's point of view. No. 2 *Neptune* and No. 3 *Wild Goose* were designed after an old side-wheeler and hot air balloon respectively. All were powered by diesel-electric engines, and the four-coach trains had a capacity of 96 passengers. The line and equipment has now been dismantled, giving Rowland Emett opportunities to ride other little railways like the Talyllyn (see Chapter VIII). But his comic fancy lives on in the pages of *Punch* and that Far Tottering line where solemn engineers wield oil cans in the shape of tea pots. . . .

Lancaster and Chester Park Railroad

On the main line there is always a destination. Otherwise how could it attract fare-paying passengers and freight? But there sometimes comes a time in the life of a Class I railroad when the engineers temporarily cease to be practitioners of the standard gauge steam loco-

No. 2 *Neptune* of Rowland Emett's "Far Tottering and Oyster Creek Railway."
She was designed with an old paddle steamer in mind and blended perfectly
with the nautical flavor of the Oyster Creek station.

Lavoy Studio

Still chugging along the rails of the 18″ gauge Lancaster and Chester Railroad,
three 50-year-old Cagney locomotives prove the sturdiness of their breed. Here,
resting on the turntable in the company park, is engine No. 45. The turntable
is supported at mid-point on old cannon balls from the Civil War.

motives and diesels and turn their thoughts to the steam trails of yesterday. Suddenly they see life from the cab footplate of the miniature railway and realize what a grand public relations gesture it would be for their own big road.

It happened on the Lancaster and Chester Railroad in South Carolina in 1946. Management decided to take that journey back in time to the heyday of the live steamer and thus remind people of the part it played in the making of America. The Junior Lancaster and Chester Park Railroad is a direct result of this thinking. The little railway was built, 1012 feet long, eleven miles from Lancaster on the Catawba River, in Springs Recreation Park.

It is a matter of history that the original mainline came into successful operation only after a long period of financial difficulty. It was built in spasms, when finance permitted, and only reached Lancaster in 1883. It was a narrow gauge line; and one of the serious economic problems was the cost of shifting all freight between narrow gauge and standard gauge cars at connecting points. In 1902, the Lancaster and Chester borrowed $125,000 from the Southern Railway and the whole narrow gauge shortline was altered to standard gauge. The old equipment was sold and standard gauge motive power and rolling stock purchased. That was the turning point. Thereafter, the road emerged from the red into the ranks of successful and profitable railroad enterprises.

It was when considerations of economy dictated conversion to diesel power that the engineers turned their thoughts to the place of the live steamer in the modern world. Did the live steamer have a useful part to play? Anybody who thinks about this subject knows that the part it can play is both useful and salutary. Ferris wheels, a swimming beach, clubhouse facilities and power-driven pool boats are available to the railroad's employees and their friends, but the chief attraction in Springs Recreation Park is the miniature railway.

Motive power is supplied by three 2200-lb., Cagney-built live steamers. These went to the Lancaster shops when purchased for major overhaul. Two of them had operated at the Charleston, South Carolina, Exposition in 1902. At the shops crown sheets were renewed, front and back flue sheets and several sections of boiler barrel and fire boxes were rebuilt. New cylinders were cast, machined and fitted. All three locomotives have slide valves and Nos. 43 and 44 have Stephenson's valve gear, while No. 45 has Walschaert gear.

Rolling stock includes four double-truck, open-top coaches 12 ft. 6 in. long and 3 ft. 10 in. wide which seat eight adults or twelve chil-

"Billy" Jones and his 18-inch gauge, oil burning steam locomotive.

Lavoy Studio

Here stands all the motive power of the 18" gauge Lancaster and Chester beside the lake along whose shores stretch the diminutive rails.

dren. The wheels are 10″ in diameter. There is also one double-truck caboose and a double-truck flat car.

Train operation is a serious business on the Junior Lancaster and Chester. As many as 45 train departures have been made in one day. One locomotive pulls three coaches, sometimes four, from the Lancaster depot which boasts a platform and four gates. As a safety measure the platform has been built so that children cannot slip between it and the trains.

There are seven switch stands, seven frogs and three switch points, a roundhouse with four tracks 18 feet long and a 60-gallon water tank. The turntable revolves on old discarded cannon balls from the Civil War. All this is made as standard main line equipment; and as the little Cagneys puff through the charming tract of woodland and water the illusion of a minuscule railroad world is complete. We are seeing the old swimming hole as we used to see it, not as a returned voyager with scales of disenchantment on his eyes. The shining rails stretch out ahead of us, reaching to eternity. There is no destination for the little, ballast-bouncing live steamers, nor for us. We sway round curves and whistle at grade crossings. Time is standing still and we are at last one with the engineer who from the cab footplate pilots his charges along the right-of-way of the miniature railway system he created.

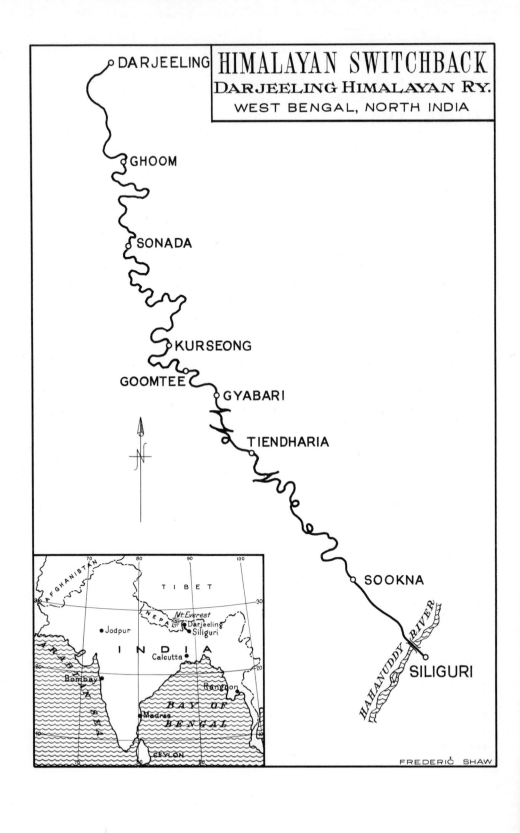

HIMALAYAN SWITCHBACK
DARJEELING HIMALAYAN RY.
WEST BENGAL, NORTH INDIA

DARJEELING

GHOOM

SONADA

KURSEONG

GOOMTEE

GYABARI

TIENDHARIA

N

SOOKNA

SILIGURI

Hahanuddy River

TIBET

AFGHANISTAN

NEPAL

Mt.Everest

Darjeeling

Siliguri

Jodpur

INDIA

Calcutta

HIMALAYA

Bombay

Rangoon

BAY OF BENGAL

Madras

CEYLON

FREDERIC SHAW

CHAPTER XIX

HIMALAYAN SWITCHBACK

The Darjeeling-Himalayan Railway

CHEGA, AN AUSTRIAN ENGINEER, was reputedly the first to apply the principle of artificially lengthening a railway line by looping in order to flatten the gradients. His Semmering line over the Eastern Alps in Europe, the first mountain railway in the world, formed a pattern for construction on the two-foot gauge line from Siliguri to Darjeeling in India, a distance of fifty-one miles.

To Franklin Presage, agent of the East Bengal Railway, goes the credit for preparing the scheme in 1878, and for completing construction in two years. The little road passes through different climatic zones in its climb from practically sea level to a height of nearly 7,000 feet and offers a variety of scenery unsurpassed by any other railway. At Darjeeling itself, the most spectacular rim of white peaks in the world greets the visitor's eye. Everest and Kanchenjunga are but two landmarks of what is known locally as "The Snows".

With Chega's principles in mind, the engineers took advantage of a military road which followed the contours of the steep Himalayan slopes. The first 7¼ miles from Siliguri are relatively easy, being laid at a 3.5 percent grade. But from that point the grades are constant and severe. The next ten miles threads a magnificent forest of sal trees rising from the tea gardens and paddy fields. As the track twists out of ravines and ascends the mountains, giant fir, the buttressed semul, palms, giant bamboo entwined with creepers, float past the windows of the smooth-running cars. On reaching an altitude of 3,000 feet, the mountain sides are scaled by fig, screw pine, oak and chestnut. Above 4,000 feet the birch and maple take over. At still higher elevations, tall oaks and walnuts are draped with lichens, orchids and mosses. Growing wild in the greatest profusion are magnolias, hydrangeas and rhododendrons. Nowhere else can be seen in one journey of a few hours such a kaleidoscope of luxuriant vegetation, primeval forest and sublime mountain peaks. It is sometimes difficult to believe that a nar-

Paul Darrell Collection

One of the loops on the Darjeeling-Himalayan Railway which with switchbacks have altogether eliminated the need for tunnels. The narrow gauge railway in its climb from Siliguri at sea level to altitudes of 7,000 feet commands unsurpassed views and a variety of flora unknown on any other two-foot-gauge line.

N.E. Frontier Railways

Darjeeling terminal is nearly seven thousand feet above sea level and provides views of Himalayan peaks such as Everest and Kanchenjunga.

Darjeeling-Himalayan Railway under construction in 1880. A good military road provided the track bed for the 2-foot-gauge railway.

Setting out for Darjeeling on the most spectacular mountain railway in the world. The train is hauled by a "B" class locomotive whose tractive effort insures safe steaming up 4 per cent grades with a load of fifty tons. Her weight is 14 tons.

N.E. Frontier Railways

The Batasia loops where the Darjeeling-Himalayan Railway makes two complete turns and gains 140 feet of vertical rise in the process. Terraced in foreground are tea gardens.

Paul Darrell Collection

Switchback on the Darjeeling-Himalayan Railway. This device to attain elevation was borrowed from American railroad practice. The train enters a dead-end from which it is reversed up another grade into another dead-end, whence it goes forward on its journey. The line has four such switchbacks.

row gauge railway can command such climatic change; and the traveler can only get out at Kurseong (elevation 4,864 feet), where the train usually stops for a luncheon break, and marvel at the intrepid little railway. The engines are coaled and watered, the ashpan emptied and the fire cleaned. Then, seemingly refreshed, the little steamers puff up the next leg of the journey to Darjeeling.

To prevent the grades, which average 4 percent, from becoming impossible, the little pike follows the devious route of the road as planned by Franklin Presage. One device to attain elevation which has been borrowed from American practice, is a switchback, the train entering a dead end, from which it is reversed up another grade into another dead end, whence it goes forward on its journey. There are four such switchbacks. There are also four spirals or loops in which the line winds along the spurs of the hills. One of these is particularly noteworthy, as in this instance the little pike makes two complete turns within a small area and gains 140 feet of vertical rise in the process. The need for tunnels was completely eliminated by this use of loops and switchbacks. It has been estimated that the use of the Government's military road, avoiding tunnels, excavations and bridges on the mountain section saved the railway company approximately $9,600 per mile at the time of building.

There is, in fact, only one bridge of note throughout the whole fifty-one miles of track and that is the seven-span bridge over the Mahanuddy River, one mile north of Siliguri.

Motive power originally employed was very small, even for a two-foot gauge railway. The original class, of 0-4-0 type, had modified diamond stacks and were replaced as loads got heavier, by a second series known as "A" and "B"'. The former series of engines had tanks located beneath the boiler barrel between the frames, and small tanks underneath the cylinders at the head end. They were built by Sharp, Stewart & Co. of Manchester, England, had outside cylinders 10 inches in diameter by 14 inches stroke, coupled wheels of 2' 2" diameter occupying a wheel base of 4' 3" and weighed 12 tons in working order.

The "B" class, which emerged from the shops of the same builder, had wheels of 2' 6" diameter and weighed 14 tons. Unique features of these little engines include a short "pannier" tank straddling the boiler behind the steam dome; a saddle tank between the dome and the smokestack; and two small tanks on either side below the cylinders. Still in service, they are extremely powerful little locomotives and can haul a load of 50 tons up a 4 percent grade. Both series were equipped with Walschaerts valve gear.

The original class of Himalayan locomotive, which had modified diamond stacks, was replaced by the second series known as "A" and "B". The engine illustrated is of the "A" class. Tanks are located beneath the boiler barrel between the frames and small tanks beneath the cylinders at the head end.

The immemorial bullock trains of India assisting in the construction of the Darjeeling-Himalayan Railway.

In 1911, the Darjeeling-Himalayan Railway received a notable addition to its locomotive stud in the shape of an 0-4-0-4-0 Garratt locomotive built by Beyer, Peacock & Co. of Gorton. It had four cylinders 11-inch by 14-inch, driving the two sets of coupled wheels, which are of 2′ 2″ diameter. The boiler had a heating surface of 667 sq. ft. and a grate area of 17.5 sq. ft. She weighed 28 tons.

The Garratt system of design was well adapted to meet the demands of the little Himalayan pike with its sharp reverse curves, the proper super-elevation for which implies that the leading and trailing axles of the engines must frequently be in different planes. The design provided extreme flexibility to the trucks in every direction, and at the same time allowed a boiler of relatively large dimensions and weight to be carried low and in a manner calculated to give a minimum of stress to the engine in negotiating sharp and reversed curves. Water and coal were carried on the truck frames, the leading truck having a tank to hold 400 gallons, while the trailing truck carried a combined tank and bunker with capacities for 200 gallons of water and one ton of coal. In addition to the two tanks already mentioned, there was a wide flat tank below the boiler barrel, holding 250 gallons, thus bringing the storage capacity to a total of 850 gallons.

Two rectangular boxes were fitted in the front of locomotives for carrying sand. During the monsoon period when as much as 125 inches of rainfall is experienced, sand is sprinkled by hand on the track.

The original passenger cars were mere 4-wheel trolleys, fitted up with benches and canvas awnings. It was an extremely uncomfortable way of traveling during the monsoon, but when one considers their horse-drawn contemporaries, the tongas, and the sheer precipices of the old military road, the awning-covered four-wheel trolleys seemed as safe as Delhi fort! Existing rolling stock includes cars 26 ft. long by 6 ft. 9 in. wide which ride with the utmost smoothness.

India today still has 3,000 miles of narrow gauge railway, so economically suited to the tasks for which it was built that little likelihood exists there will be any considerable widening of the gauge. It conforms to many of the early principles laid down that the feeder lines for Class I railroads should be of light construction and unencumbered by a load of debt. The Darjeeling-Himalayan Railway enjoys, it goes without saying, a big tourist traffic in the "cold weather", and also a large tea and general merchandise traffic.

Since the partition of India the little Himalayan road has been extended 95 miles, and as from January 15, 1958, grouped with part of

A general view of the Darjeeling-Himalayan Railway which provides for the traveler such a variety of mountain scenery and climatic change as could be found on no other railroad in the world.

Kurseong Station (elevation 4,864 feet) where the little Siliguri-Darjeeling train stops to debark passengers for a luncheon break. Throughout most of its length the 2-foot-gauge Darjeeling-Himalayan Railway makes good use of the old military road, thereby having saved an estimated $9,600 per mile in construction costs.

the Bengal-Assam Railway system under the new Northeast Frontier Railway, with headquarters in Pandu. The creation of this new zonal railway administration, though small in size in comparison with other Indian units, was necessitated by manifold considerations — strategic, administrative and operational. It is deemed to be of vital importance that there should be a dependable, continuous and all-weather line between the Eastern frontier and the rest of India. That the Darjeeling-Himalayan Railway and its extension will play its part in this new zonal system goes without saying.

India has come a long way since Independence and is providing an increasing amount of her own motive power, rolling stock and equipment. The Chittaranjan Locomotive Works produced 156 heavy locomotives in 1956-57 and is expected to produce 168 during 1957-58. The output of the Integral Coach Factory at Perambur, which was 88 unfinished coaches in 1956-57, is expected to rise to 180 this year and 285 for the year 1958-59.

Historically, no country in the world has taken more advantage of economical means of railway transportation than India, or has made a better adaptation of different gauges as a means to an end. In that great sub-continent there is the broad 5 ft. 6 in. gauge running through the main arteries of traffic. With the broad gauge, there are first-class meter gauge lines, of which there are now 15,000 miles, carrying less traffic per mile in less populated areas. Last but not least and resisting any pressures for standardization, are the hill railways of narrow gauge, the Queen of them all, the Himalayan-Darjeeling Railway as permanent a "fixture" of the high hills as any steam-hauled two-footer can be in this modern world.

HENRY GREENLY
1876-1947

W. J. BASSETT-LOWKE, founder of the firm
that bears his name.

ALBERT S. CAMPBELL is probably the pioneer
commercial manufacturer of model live steam
scale locomotives in America. A fine mechanic,
he invented many labor saving attachments for
his own use.

Mr. Claret in his home workshop. He is typical
of the fine old craftsmen whose skill produced
most accurate and finished machine parts. Their
work contributed to the success and reputation
of Bassett-Lowke, Ltd.

CHAPTER XX

MINIATURE GALLERY

Albert S. Campbell—Wenman J. Bassett-Lowke—
Henry Greenly—P. S. Sturtevant—E. O. Thornton—
Robert H. Butler—Albert J. Wagner—Ken S. Williams

EVERY CRAFT AND profession has its own picture gallery of eminent men who have contributed something of lasting value over the years. The miniature railways of the world have been well served in this respect by a number of outstanding mechanical minds, some long since unhappily passed from the scene and some still experimenting with and perfecting little live steamers and diesels. A miniature gallery of some of these personalities and what they did, or are doing, seems a fitting finale to this volume.

Diesel motive power on miniature railways has been growing in professional and public acceptance; and it would be picayunish of the traveler on the little railways who, though he prefers steam, ignores the capabilities and value of diesel power. Has the advent of the diesel locomotive, now in almost universal use on American main lines, pushed the steam locomotive completely from the scene? Is the diesel's efficiency so incontrovertibly proven that soon the live steamer will be as outmoded as the clipper ship?

There is no denying the almost instant availability of the internal combustion engine; but the replacement costs of the diesel, owing to a shorter life expectancy than the steam locomotive, has raised doubts about its over-all economy. There are many men in railroading today who believe there may be a resurgence of thinking back towards the live steamer, not as the old-timers knew it but developed along entirely new lines when steam will really come into its own.

However that may be, no attempt will be made in this miniature gallery to editorialize on the relative merits of the two types of motive power. The men so honored can speak for themselves.

Pioneer Manufacturer

Chronologically, one of the first men in the gallery to make his influence felt in miniature railroading was Albert S. Campbell, now eighty-five years of age. A onetime employee of the Brooklyn Elevated Railroad, he was a messenger in the Master Mechanics office at the age of thirteen. Moving after two years to the locomotive shops, Mr. Camp-

This 1″-scale American type steam locomotive was built in 1898 by A. S. Campbell from the set of castings he developed to sell commercially. A few extras such as the dummy air pump, jamb brakes between the drivers and the marker lamps have been added. The engine and tender sold in 1902 for $145 finished and ready to run.

A three-quarter-inch scale non-working model of a Beyer-Peacock Garratt type locomotive built for exhibition purposes by the famed firm of model-makers Messrs. Bassett-Lowke of Northampton, England. This type of locomotive is used extensively in South Africa.

bell served an apprenticeship of four years. At the age of seventeen, he was working from 6:50 A.M. to 9:00 P.M. (including Sundays and Holidays) at the Long Island Railroad shops. Mr. Campbell laconically states that he left the road after one year because "the hours were too long." Much of the rest of his life, until retirement in 1939, was spent in the machine shops of the elevated railroads of New York and Brooklyn.

In 1894, Mr. Campbell permitted his strong leanings towards the miniature steam locomotive to express themselves in the building of scale models, and his entrance into the field commercially came in the closing year of the Old Century. Adopting the famed No. 870 of the old New York Central and Hudson River RR, Mr. Campbell devised patterns for castings in three sizes: $3\frac{3}{16}$-inch-gauge; $4\frac{3}{4}$-inch-gauge; and $6\frac{1}{2}$-inch-gauge. Over the years he sold more than one hundred sets of these castings. His final version of No. 870 were patterns in $12\frac{5}{8}$-inch-gauge and he had two sets of castings made, one of which he sold to a man in Pennsylvania and the other is still in his possession. So far as is known, this was the first small-scale, live steam commercial enterprise in the United States.

Mr. Campbell still has intact all his patterns for these small-scale locomotives. It is to be hoped they may one day be put to good use in the fabrication of further versions of handsome old No. 870. The pioneer's mind is still as alert as ever; and nothing would give him greater pleasure than to feel his early experiments are still of value to the live steam enthusiast. He deserves a special place in the Miniature Gallery.

Passport to Lilliput

Second in point of chronology is a household name in the world of live steam models—Basset-Lowke. Young Wenman J. Basset-Lowke was apprenticed to his father's engineering works in Northampton, England, in the last decade of the Nineteenth Century. He had a friend in the firm's accounting office, Harry F. R. Franklin. Technical training and accounting was a happy combination for two young men who long had had in mind a business of their own devoted to model railways and ships.

Frustrated by the difficulty of getting well designed components, they were given access to the shop equipment and made their own. Basset-Lowke Senior permitted them to display these products in the Company's store window. Promoting their modest efforts by advertising in the columns of *The Model Engineer*, a newly established journal

A 2-inch scale, 9½-inch-gauge L.N.E.R. Atlantic type steam locomotive built by Bassett-Lowke around 1935. This size locomotive proved very popular over England for use in gardens where there was sufficient room for a substantial length of track.

This 1886 photograph depicts the Northampton plant owned by the couple standing before the door. They are Mr. and Mrs. Bassett, grandparents of the small boy on their left who is the future model parts manufacturer, Mr. W. J. Basset-Lowke.

edited by the late Percival Marshall, the partners soon realized how widespread was the demand for model railway components. A mail order business was soon built up.

Thus was the firm of Basset-Lowke born, a fact crystalized in the first catalogue issued in 1899. The catalog was unusual in that it resorted not to the usual half-tone illustrations but to actual small photographs laboriously pasted on to the pages.

Percival Marshall's venture into the model engineer publication field coincided with the early beginnings of Basset-Lowke. *The Model Engineer* naturally made much of this new hobby; and to the present day it is recognized as the Bible of the fraternity.

In 1900, Mr. Basset-Lowke visited the Paris Exposition and discovered miniature steam locomotives of revolutionary design. They were fabricated with a precision unknown in the so-called "toy" engines. On his return to England he fashioned designs for British locomotives which he sent over to French manufacturers for interpretation into finished models. Thereafter, he and his colleagues made a sharp distinction between a model locomotive and a toy.

The Paris venture brought Mr. Basset-Lowke into contact with the late Stefan Bing whose Nuremberg firm built the impressive exhibit at the French Exposition. Mr. Bing was commissioned to build from Basset-Lowke designs steam models of the British *Black Prince*, a 4-4-0 type with a 6-wheel tender. This was the first attempt of a Continental firm to build a British model live steamer. It was an immediate success in England and the precursor of other fine model engines.

In 1902, Mr. Basset-Lowke formed an association with Henry Greenly who in designing the first 3-inch scale locomotive Basset-Lowke ever built ushered in a new era for the model railroader. This handsome miniature was the 4-6-2 *Colossus* which is worthy of a chapter all on its own. Built for Captain Howey's Staughton Manor Railway at 15-inch-gauge, the *Colossus* saw service on the Ravenglass and Eskdale Railway in Cumberland.

The large-scale model building operation has now been discontinued but in other fields the scope of this pioneer Northampton firm's activities has been widened. From locomotives it was but a small step into the marine world of models. Parts were fashioned for a substantial list of ship fittings from deck to engine room. Basset-Lowke assembled ship models from the famous *Mauretania*, which held the blue ribbon of the Atlantic for twenty-one years, to the ½-inch-scale model of the *Queen Elizabeth*. Model making has even been expanded into large

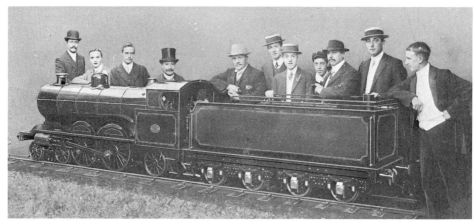

Whether the group of interested human beings or the locomotive is the prime interest in this photograph seems open to debate. Also, whether the gentleman in the silk topper or the one leaning on the cab in a possessory pose is the proud owner, it is now too late to discover. In any event, the *Green Dragon* 15-inch-gauge steam locomotive is No. 16 on the builder's roster and it would appear that Mr. Henry Greenly, second from the right, had considerable to do with it in behalf of the Bassett-Lowke builder.

The first 3-inch scale Pacific type (4-6-2) steam locomotive ever built. It was designed and built by Bassett-Lowke, Ltd. of Northampton, England for Capt. J. E. P. Howey for his Stoughton Manor Railway. This engine was later sold to the Ravenglass & Eskdale Ry. of Cumberland.

working models of power stations, whiskey distilleries, water works and model cities, such as Coventry which was razed by bombing attack during World War II and for the rebuilding of which a 50-square-foot model was made.

Mr. Basset-Lowke is still active in the affairs of the firm. It is written that the mischievousness of youth is still in his blood, "making him a kind of Peter Pan." It is possible that the Boy Who Never Grew Up is the closest kin of the model railroader!

Henry Greenly: A Memoir

Because he was so closely associated with Basset-Lowke of Northampton, the place for Henry Greenly in the miniature gallery is here, close to his old friend. Mr. Greenly was chief engineer of the Ravenglass and Eskdale Railway in Cumberland, England, and engineer of the Romney, Hythe and Dymchurch Light Railway in Kent. No designer has had more influence on the 15-inch-gauge miniature railways in England and the United States. His accomplishments in railroad engineering and other engineering crafts have been mentioned throughout this book and are too well known to detail here. The following are passages contributed in a memoir by his daughter, Mrs. Eleanor Howard Steel of Princes Risborough, England:

"There was no malice in Father's makeup. He made a few enemies as a man of his personality would be likely to do: and because he had an Edwardian sense of fun and his generation's liking for practical jokes, he was prone to bait any overt enemy who provoked him too much. If there was one thing he disliked in his fellow humans it was pretentiousness, and technical pretentiousness most of all. . . .

"He was of an economical turn of mind and money didn't worry him overly much; and as a result there was never a great deal of it. He liked fame, but not power; and the financial side of his life was not of paramount importance to him. He never cared very much for personal adornment and dearly loved to work in very old clothes. . . .

"He was very fond of an artist's brown overall supplemented by footwear of bizzarre character, a pair of old white buckskin cricket boots. I can remember a projected visit from Captain Howey when the Romney, Hythe and Dymchurch Railway was in its early stages, and my father being persuaded to change into more respectable garb, only as the visit failed to materialize, changing back to the old, comfortable clothing—to be caught thus by Captain Howey!

"My brother is very like my father in build, voice and in his mannerisms. An old member of Basset-Lowke, meeting him recently

E. O. Thornton

The sturdy, popular American type, 12-inch-gauge live steam locomotive built by Elmer O. Thornton of Des Moines, Iowa, who has ingeniously captured an arresting name for his product by calling it a "STEAMLINER." For several years he has been kept busy turning out these efficient amusement park locomotives.

Robert D. Beach

Indicative of the trend away from steam driven amusement park trains is this handsome two-unit streamliner each with its own gasoline motor. It is a G-16 type manufactured by the Allan Herschell Co., Inc. of North Tonawanda, N.Y. The company also manufactures a smaller, single unit called the G-12. They operate on 16″ and 12″ gauge track respectively and have proven popular all over the country. The steam locomotive is a Great Northern Ry. Pacific, given to the local community.

and not knowing him as a boy, was quite startled; he said it gave him quite a turn when Kenneth came into the room—it was like my father being back."

The Day of the Diesels

There are many children growing up today to whom the miniature live steamer is an attractive little vagrant, more amusing than realistic in terms of the main line. These children are products of the diesel age and take readily to the miniature streamliners in amusement parks all over the country.

One of the men most worthy of inclusion in the diesel miniature gallery is Mr. P. S. Sturtevant of Glen Ellyn, Illinois. In the early days of the depression of the 'Thirties he set out to transform his backyard into a model railroader's paradise. His son was too young to appreciate a miniature railway, but provided the moral justification for turning many years of leisure time to the completion of such a system! Although of live steamer design, the first motive power unit was electric powered and hauled authentic freight cars to accommodate passengers. It is said that the son, Lee, grew up to appreciate the little road but was permitted to work the motive power only when his father was around. This has been the perennial treatment of sons for whom model railroads were created!

Mr. Sturtevant's backyard miniature system soon caught the attention of a successful Chicago merchant who saw the immense possibilities of a miniature train in his store at Christmas time. Since the diesel streamliner was just then moving on to the transportation scene, Mr. Sturtevant designed a miniature diesel unit powered by electricity. It was such a success in the department store that he was prompted to form a manufacturing company with Mr. R. D. Robertson. The organization was known as the Miniature Train Company, located at Addison, Illinois. After many years of successful operation in department stores, another diesel-type streamliner was designed, this time powered with small, air-cooled gasoline engines for carnivals and amusement parks. These gasoline-powered units were manufactured in quantity and soon became known as "Addison Trains."

By 1946, the demand for the "Addison Trains" had become so great that a bigger location was required and the Miniature Train Company moved to a specially constructed plant at Rensselaer, Indiana. Mr. Sturtevant was constantly seeking to improve his product and embarked on a larger, more ambitious miniature train. The diesel type streamliner had proved so popular, the aid of the Electro-Motive

Mr. Robert H. Butler of Santa Rosa, California, and his beautiful 12-inch-gauge Atlantic type (4-4-2) steam locomotive which he designed and built. All the drawings for this engine are available in loose-leaf form.

Another contrast in the modern trend. Allan Herschell Co's. single unit 16-inch-gauge streamliner standing beside a Santa Fe streamliner.

Division of General Motors Corporation was enlisted. General Motors furnished blueprints and specifications of their F-7 diesel locomotive and coaches, with the result that the now famous G-16 miniature trains, constructed to exact detail at $\frac{1}{5}$ scale, are now operating on a 16-inch-gauge track in amusement parks throughout the country.

In November 1956, the Miniature Train Company of Rensselaer, Indiana, merged with the Allan Herschell Company of North Tonawanda, New York. In their respective fields, each of these companies was the largest manufacturer in the world of outdoor amusement equipment—the former in trains and the latter in merry-go-rounds and other amusement rides. It is a far call from Mr. Sturtevant's back yard to North Tonawanda where the giant merger is turning out the majority of the factory-constructed miniature trains in operation today. But this is the day of the diesel, and more handsome and efficient motive power units for miniature railways would be hard to find.

Iowan Steamliner

A fresh "copy" slant has been given to his advertising by an Iowan miniature locomotive builder in the use of the word *steamliner* as distinguished from *streamliner*. Mr. E. O. Thornton of Des Moines, Iowa, has been manufacturing 12-inch-gauge live steamers for many years and his imaginative approach to promoting steam has paid off in a very busy shop.

He departs from orthodox practice in the use of inside steam chests—those placed under the saddle and between the cylinders. Excellent as this may be from the mechanical standpoint, it leaves much to be desired from the viewpoint of design. Efficiency, however, is undoubtedly improved since this positioning tends to insulate the chests and reduce heat loss, an important factor. Model railroading tends to develop highly individualistic approaches to specific problems and the engineers who create these little railways become "characters" in the old and honorable sense of the word. For this reason, Mr. Thornton rates a special place in the Miniature Gallery.

Engraver's Engine

A California engraver has forsaken his acids and etching tools for the machine tools of the model railroader and has fabricated a fine small replica of the Southern Pacific's old Atlantic type locomotive. Moreover, once under steam, the engraver reversed processes and remade all his scale drawings in the most meticulous detail, made engraver's plates and had them printed—to form one of the most carefully prepared sets of working drawings ever encountered.

This 12″ gauge *Lady Baltimore* 4-4-4 is another handsome product of the Wagner shops. Precision built, it has power, speed and a grace seldom encountered in small, park-type steam locomotives. It is lacquered in a rich Washington blue, striped and lettered in gold leaf.

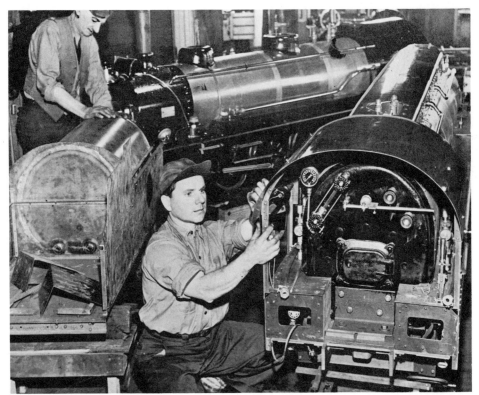

Mr. Albert J. Wagner and his son busily at work putting the finishing touches on some 16″ gauge steam locomotives in their shop at Plainfield, Illinois.

The engraver, Mr. Robert H. Butler of Santa Rosa, some years ago first tackled a 2½-inch-gauge Mountain type (4-8-2) model by buying commercial castings. It was tested under steam and operated successfully. Mr. Butler was now ready for his main project—the designing and building of a 12-inch-gauge live steamer.

The engine was designed to a scale of 2 inches to one foot (9½-inch-gauge); but to lower the center of gravity the track gauge was widened to twelve inches. Detailed drawings were made, the parts fashioned and the actual construction begun. The result of Mr. Butler's labors was as near a perfect replica of the old No. 3000 type, Southern Pacific 4-4-2 as has appeared in a decade.

Unhappily, the powers of the little Atlantic miniature have never been realized. Due to illness, Mr. Butler has taken this little railway no further than the motive power which lies in storage awaiting an uncertain destiny.

Wagnerian Opus

Another engineer who has developed a highly individualistic approach to miniature railways is Albert J. Wagner of Plainfield, Illinois. His locomotives are distinguished by a pleasing streamlined design which follows no known prototype. Their characteristics have proved to have great commercial value, for his shop is busy with orders from all over the United States and from places as far-away as Africa.

Mr. Wagner's shop capacity is about ten locomotives annually but his actual output is less since skilled labor in the little Plainfield community is at a premium and he likes to keep it a family business. He can build to order miniature live steamers ranging from 2½-inch-gauge (costing around $1,500) to 24-inch-gauge (costing around $30,000). The accompanying illustrations are typical of the fine design of the Wagnerian version of the miniature locomotive builder's craft.

"Just Like a Big One"

A relative newcomer to the field of miniature locomotive building is Mr. "Ken" S. Williams of Wyano, Pennsylvania, proprietor of the Crown Metal Products Company. A strong devotee of steam, he has always been animated by a desire to make his products available to the railroad enthusiast in the average income bracket. For this reason, Mr. Williams has set himself the task of making his little live steamers very competitive in price.

His attractive American-type 4-4-0's are reminiscent of the general outlines of the Cagney product. It is no idle claim that his "coal-

Author's Collection

Red Devil No. 5000 is a Wagner 14″ gauge live steamer operating in River-view Park near Chicago. Lettering and striping are in gold leaf on a two-tone red lacquer finish.

K. S. Williams

A newcomer to the field of small-gauge steam locomotive manufacture is Mr. Kenneth S. Williams pictured here driving his American type locomotive No. 31, his builder's No. 1, 15½″ gauge. These locomotives are assembled at Wyano, Penn.

burning, live steam locomotive sounds, smells, looks and handles just like a big one." Furthermore, his product can be purchased, according to the brochure, "for less money than you would pay for a good sports car or boat."

Built to operate on a 15½-inch-gauge track, the Williams brand of live steamer is 11 feet long over all, 3 feet high at the cab roof and weighs approximately 1750 lbs. The drivers are 11 inches in diameter. Boilers are all-welded, tested to a pressure of 188 lbs., and the operating pressure is 125 lbs. Equipped with two injectors and most fittings normally a part of the main line engine, steam is raised by use of coal. The tenders provide ample space for both coal and water. Crown also manufactures passenger cars.

Envoi

It would be highly improper for the author of a book to include himself in the miniature gallery of men who have contributed much to the building of miniature railways. The author's contribution, when the pen is mightier than the machine tool, is to chronicle events as he has experienced them, in more than a half century of railroading, or to secure information from correspondents all over the world. Part of the author's experience in this *genre* of miniature railways has been to fabricate model live steamers; and without claiming a place in the gallery itself, it may not perhaps be inapposite to set down such experiences.

The author was inspired to work on his own live steamer when he first encountered Albert S. Campbell in 1900. Mr. Campbell was doing business in Monticello, New York, and it was about this time the old New York Central and Hudson River Railroad produced its interesting No. 2900 series of Atlantic type locomotives. The picture and drawings of the engine being available in the now defunct *Railway & Locomotive Engineering* magazine of New York, a start was made on a model of No. 2990. A budding draftsman, the author utilized his skills in devising the necessary drawings for a one-inch scale steam locomotive.

Wheel castings were purchased from Mr. Campbell and patterns made for other parts. Under guidance of friendly machinists, the engine began to take shape. It is sad to reflect that No. 2990 was never completed for steam trials; but it was advanced enough to satisfy the acquisitive instincts of an unscrupulous engine fancier. It vanished in 1923 without trace.

In 1946 a 9-inch-gauge, 2-inch scale American-type live steam locomotive was undertaken. This model, which took two years to

The author's 9″ gauge, coal-burning live steamer nearing completion, showing some of the boiler-head fittings. The pipe from the steam dome supplies steam for the turret head which in turn distributes steam to the several cab fittings. The tender frame is welded up of light steel channels.

Back in Wichita, Kansas, the Ottaway Company is turning out all the 12″ gauge steam locomotives it can assemble. These little machines are sturdily and practically built and have the best proportions of any commercially made in the United States.

complete, followed no specific prototype but was something of a composite of the features which had long appealed to the author. Movies of the first day's steam trials are all that remain, for the little live steamer was sold to another enthusiast.

In setting up portraits or vignettes for the miniature gallery a hundred personalities cross the author's mind. They may have built just that one live steamer; they may have organized a little railroad, like Captain J. E. P. Howey who brought the miniature railway to its very apotheosis; or they may have started something, like Arthur Heywood in the 1870's, which handed the torch of mechanical experience to men like Henry Greenly. Unfortunately, there are many others who, for divers reasons, could not be included in this book.

BILL OF LADING

This book would probably never have come into being were it not for Denis A. Rooksby. His wide experience in the field of literature was a fortuitous circumstance. As both an author and an editor he was well qualified as guide in the assembly of this book. I can but inadequately record my debt to his counsel and friendship. And fortunate are we indeed to have traveled between us most of the lines written about in this book.

Crowding the top of the list of those others to whom I wish to make grateful acknowledgement is Paul B. Darrell of Richmond, California, who made available his extensive railroad library. To George A. Barlow, senior "driver" (engineer) of the Romney, Hythe and Dymchurch Light Railway of England goes the author's gratitude for supplying most of the data and many fine photographs of that outstanding miniature railway. Similarly, Cliff B. Shirley of Prairie Village, Kansas, Edward T. Francis of Livingstone, New Jersey, combined talents as a self-styled "Cagney Club" to track down much of the data about the Brothers Cagney. A. B. "Jeff" Jefferis of Piedmont, Missouri, also had his fingers in the Cagney diggings, and Edward T. Francis of Livingston, New Jersey and John Murray of Rehoboth, Massachusetts, supplied valuable data for the scale drawings.

Richard H. Kindig, narrow gauge sage of Denver, Colorado; Henry T. Crittenden of Norfolk, Virginia, scribe of the "two-footers"; and Burton Logan, curator of the Edaville Museum, South Carver, Massachusetts, formed a trio which aided materially in assembling facts concerning the 2-foot-gauge lines. To Mr. Crittenden I am especially indebted for placing at my disposal the results of his research on the Otavi Railway of Southwest Africa.

Mr. Henry Buck of Seascale, Cumberland, England, went out of his way to shoot special pictures of the Ravenglass and Eskdale Railway and supply valuable data; while down on the Kentish coast Dr. P. Ransome-Wallis of Herne Bay kindly loaned some of his photos depicting the Romney line. My friend, Richard Pennoyer of London, brother of the late famed railroad artist, Sheldon Pennoyer, loaned photographs from his extensive collection.

Mr. Robert Stokes of the Church Information Board, London, gave much helpful advice on the general outline of the book and supplied invaluable data. And I must pass warm encomiums on the tireless efforts of different officers and members of the two railway societies, the Festiniog and the Talyllyn, in supplying photographs and information about the preservation of these two historical British railways.

Every historical writing is the handiwork of many unseen hands. To the many who go unlisted my thanks is no less real. The whole story could not possibly be encompassed within the limits of one book. There is enough material available to fill many volumes. I hope to carry on the research and set it down for further chronicles of the "LITTLE RAILWAYS OF THE WORLD."

FREDERIC SHAW, A. I. A.

Sausalito, California

BIBLIOGRAPHY

NARROW GAUGE RAILS TO PORTMADOC. J. C. Boyd. *London:* Oakwood Press

The Locomotive Railway Carriage & Wagon Review. Vols. XLVIII, 1942; XLV, 1938 and XVI, 1910.

LIGHT MINIATURE LOCOMOTIVES OF GREAT BRITAIN. Eric S. Tonks

NARROW GAUGE RAILWAYS OF GREAT BRITAIN. F. H. Howson. *London:* Ian Allan, 1948

THE VALE OF RHEIDOL RAILWAY. Compiled by Lewis Cozens. *Surrey,* England

TALYLLYN RAILWAY OFFICIAL GUIDE, 1958

WORLD'S SMALLEST PUBLIC RAILWAY. Dr. P. Ransome-Wallis. *London:* Ian Allan 1954.

THE ROMNEY, HYTHE & DYMCHURCH RAILWAY. *London:* The Locomotive Publishing Co., 1950

INDIAN RAILWAYS. Vol. I, No. 12 and Vol. II, No. 4

RAILWAYS SINCE INDEPENDENCE. *New Delhi:* Publications Division, Government of India

INDIAN RAILWAYS 1956-7. *New Delhi:* Ministry of Railways, Government of India

LIGHT RAILWAYS. J. C. Mackay, *London:* Crosby Lockwood, 1896

RAILWAY BUDGET FOR 1958-59. Shri Jagjivan Ram. *New Delhi:* Government of India Press.

THE NARROW GAUGE RAILWAYS OF WALES. R. W. Kidner. *London:* Oakwood Press, 1956

THE LYNTON & BARNSTABLE RAILWAY. L. Y. Catchpole. *London:* Oakwood Press, 1936

LIGHT & NARROW GAUGE LOCOMOTIVES. R. W. Kidner. Oakwood Press, 1949

ENGLISH NARROW GAUGE RAILWAYS. R. W. Kidner, Oakwood Press

INDIAN RAILWAYS: One Hundred Years 1853-1953. *New Delhi:* Ministry of Railways

THE TIMES of London

Chicago *TRIBUNE*

St. Louis *POST-DISPATCH*

San Francisco *NEWS*